CAPRICORN RISING

CAPRICORN RISING

PRODUCTIVE POET, SCIENTIST, MENTOR

KATHLEEN BURT

Capricorn Rising
Productive Poet, Scientist, Mentor

ISBN 978-1-926975-09-2 Paperback

Genoa House

www.genoahouse.com

books@genoahouse.com

Published simultaneously in Canada, the United Kingdom, and the United States of America. For information on obtaining permission for use of material from this work, please submit a written request to:

books@genoahouse.com

FREQUENTLY ASKED QUESTIONS

What is the Rising Sign?

It's the astrological *persona* or Mask. Technically, it's the constellation coming up over the horizon at the *time* of birth, in the *location,* the city or town where we were born. Because it's rising overhead, this constellation is also called the Ascendant.

Located on the Cusp of the First House, (Identity) the degree of the Rising Sign is our personal, symbolic place in time and space. An accurate time of birth is very important.

How does my Rising Sign differ symbolically from my Sun Sign?

Here are some technical differences to ponder:

The Sun is a star around which planets revolve. The Rising Sign is an entire constellation. The Ascendant Sign changed every two hours the day we were born, while the Sun Sign was shared with a greater number of people born within several weeks of us. The Twelve Rising constellations have different types of charisma and magnetism.

The Rising Sign is associated with dawn and new beginnings. We experience this when transits of the faster-moving planets—

Mercury, Mars, Venus or the Luminaries (the Sun and Moon) cross the Ascendant and move through our First House. With transiting Mars on the Ascendant, we may decide to sign up at the gym or take karate. With Mercury transiting, our new endeavor may be a craft class or a letter to the editor. We can follow the motion of planets across our Ascendant in the ephemeris. Slower-moving planets may influence the Ascendant for several years. We adjust, then get used to them being around and they no longer feel new.

What does the Sun symbolize in the horoscope?

You may recall from *Archetypes of the Zodiac* that for every planet there are two levels of symbolism, esoteric (spiritual) and mundane (instinctual.)

At one level, the Sun symbolizes the Ego. Symbolically, the planets in the horoscope are to the Ego as the physical Sun is to the Solar System: the Sun is the source of light and heat and the planets play a subordinate role. They represent qualities or attributes of the Sun. (Mercury symbolizes the Ego's curiosity, its ability to learn and communicate knowledge; Mars, the Ego's flight-or-fight response; assertiveness, competitive spirit, agility, coordination, passion. Venus represents the Feeling Function and the way that the Ego relates to others (preferably harmoniously, non-competitively) as well as aesthetics and the individual'sl taste.

But for those interested in spiritual symbolism, the Sun is a symbol of the Self. Its alchemical metal is gold.

Poets and storytellers through the ages have made use of the metals associated with the planets to let us know that a poem or story has a deeper message. "The Golden Fleece" alluded to in the Aries Rising chapter is such a tale, a Search for the precious treasure, the Self. William Butler Yeats, who studied astrology with the Golden Dawn Society, ended his poem, "The Song of Wandering Aengus" with the lines "...and pluck till time and times are done/the Silver Apples of the Moon/the Golden Apples of the Sun." There's a sense of eternity: "till time and times are done." Golden Apples are delicious, but actual silver ones are hard to find!

Modern seekers after "the Grail" or the "Golden Fleece" learn a great deal about themselves by hindsight after transits to the Sun by outer planets, (Saturn and beyond.) Others pass through the same transit cycles and only want to know "when will this finally end?" There are two distinct levels.

Are there different levels to the Rising Sign constellations too? Or is the Mask just a superficial face we present to the world? Just "putting our best face on things?"

Absolutely, there's a deeper level. An astrological Mask represents an entire constellation *of possibilities.* It's like owning a shelf of actor's Masks. Or we may wear a series of Masks over the years. Let's consider a constellation with a wide range of possibilities: Gemini Rising. We all know chatty, gossipy Gemini Rising people. We see Hermes-the-Trickster or Prankster in them. We've met Peter Pan and Tinkerbelle, Gemini Rising people who don't want to grow up! Jung's puer and puella. But there are also brilliant Gemini Rising people with a wry sense of humor, like Henry Kissinger; talented teachers like Marcel Marceau who opened his school of mime to preserve the Harlequin tradition. There are talented Gemini Rising craftspeople. There are Gemini Rising lecturers who seem to ramble but then surprise us by summing everything up beautifully with a power point presentation, bringing all the pieces together at the end.

Gemini Rising people can be highly intuitive, like Jeanne Dixon and Mira Alfassar Richard, The Mother of the Aurobindo Ashram in Pondicherry, India. We see this when Gemini Rising attunes not only to Hermes/Mercury but also to its esoteric ruler.

Venus rules aesthetics and values. *So many Masks* are possible for Gemini: journalist, talk show host, Advisor to the King (Kissinger) Court Jester (juggler or mime), author, teacher, psychic and more. The more spiritual Geminis seem able to reconcile the pillars of Hercules (the glyph for the Twins) in a harmonious manner. They're attuned to Venus, the principal of harmony.

Is it true that the Rising Sign, not the Sun Sign is what people usually come up with at parties when they try to guess your Sign? They see the Mask?

Yes, that happens fairly often. Most of us prepare our party-going-Mask carefully; we put thought and attention into it. Still, the Mask will reflect the planet close to the Rising Sign if we have one there. Uranus near the Ascendant, or contracting it, usually means a zany choice of apparel, Saturn near the Ascendant tends towards a businesslike, serious Mask. The look is "classic"—often black or the latest "new black." The briefcase is left home but the wallet or purse contains business cards in case they're needed. Mars near the Ascendant: elegant sportswear to show off a buff body. Venus near the Ascendant: style; a sense of color that accentuates the hair, the eyes, the complexion or hides flaws. Moon near the Ascendant may discuss an "ex" or a close family member they're concerned about, their pet, or, worst case-scenario, their dreadful "ex" at the party. Whether or not the person is a nurturer, they appear to be.

Here's where the confusion occurs: a person might guess "Libra Rising" when Venus is on the Ascendant in some other Rising Sign. Or guess "Cancer Rising" when the Moon is on the Ascendant, regardless of Rising Sign. The businesslike person would seem like Capricorn Rising because Saturn's on the Ascendant. If any of these planets were in the middle of the First House, they'd still affect the magnetism but to a lesser degree.

Are First House Planets part of the Mask, or just the Rising Sign Degree and the planet closest to it?

The entire First House is part of the Mask, including all its planets. Twelfth House planets within five degrees of the Rising Sign influence the Mask, too.

Each planet in the First House contributes something of its own nature to our magnetism. With Saturn-in-the-First House, others probably see you as a responsible, well-organized person, disciplined, and focused. This will draw you a lot of work! By the age of

30, you'd most likely be hard on yourself as a result of your perceptions about *others* unfulfilled expectations of you. (Perhaps parents and mentors never really expected that of you! It's *your* First House Saturn, after all, not theirs!) At work, you've come to believe, "the buck stops here" on your desk. Or, with Mars in your First, you see yourself as an active person, (you were probably athletic in youth) but by now, at 55, your may feel frustrated because you no longer have the physical stamina or agility you had at 35. Or you may forget this on occasion, overexert yourself and pull a muscle or develop a hernia.

So, the Mask not only symbolizes how others see us; it *also colors how we perceive ourselves.* It's possible to over-identify with First House planets after Midlife. Our First House Saturn keeps overachieving but we may no longer enjoy our jobs. Or, our First House Moon still wears an outdated Supermom Mask. Wearing a Mask that no longer serves often interferes with drawing new friends or participating in activities that we would now enjoy. Our days are filled with people who wear old Masks, like ours.

The Venus-in-the-First House sorority girl or Adonis-the-handsome-salesman particularly feel a sense of loss as beauty fades after Midlife. For Mercury-in the-First House, multi-tasking becomes more difficult. (With aging they're more forgetful.) The Masks that worked for us in youth become difficult to maintain; we invest more and more energy in keeping their veneer fresh and shiny as the decades pass.

How can I find my Rising Sign? And how can I find out if I have any First House planets?

The information you need for calculating your horoscope, including the Rising Sign and the houses is on your birth certificate. If you don't have a copy, it's available from the Department of Vital Statistics in the capitol of the state where you were born.

A word of caution, though. Some states have two-page certificates with the time of birth on the second page. So, it's a good idea to ask, "is there is a second page?" when you call to order it. If so, do request both pages. Otherwise, they may send only the first page. If the time of birth is missing, you'll have only half the information. (If you know your latitude and longitude, you'll know your symbolic place in space but not in time.) Once you have the information, you can proceed to an internet site and fill in the data or see an astrologer for a private session. If you have a serious interest in calculating many horoscopes, software is available for purchase through Solar Fire, Matrix or Astrolabe.

What if I don't have any First House Planets?

Don't worry about it. Not everyone has a planet sitting right on his Ascendant or in the First House. Planets in other houses will likely make contacts (aspects) to the Ascendant degree. Novelist Simone de Beauvoir and psychologist Sigmund Freud didn't have any.

First look for the planet or planets that rule your Rising Sign. Simone de Beauvoir had Scorpio Rising.

Scorpio has two ruling planets. One of them, Mars, trined the Ascendant from the Fifth House; she was passionate about Life.

The other ruler of Scorpio, Pluto was in her Seventh, long-term relationships, in an unstable aspect (inconjunct) to the Ascendant.

John Paul Sartre, the love of her life for fifty years, put her through a great deal with his many love affairs, about which he wrote her in great detail (in spite of her objections that she didn't care to be in the bedroom as a voyeur.) Also painful were his doubts about Existentialism, the philosophy of personal freedom by which they'd both lived their lives, in his later years. But his adopting a young woman as his "literary heir" and advisor, a position that she'd previously held herself, was probably the greatest shock.

The major theme of the Mask and the obstacles it faces; the adjustments that must be made are described.

Next, look for *any* planet that contacts *the Ascendant degree* to learn about your Mask. Beauvoir's Moon and Saturn in Pisces were conjunct her Fifth House Mars. They were in a nice free-flowing trine to the Ascendant; she was Sartre's anchor (when he tired of a lover or the woman became too demanding, Simone got rid of her for him, because she said "we had spoiled Sartre; he didn't like unpleasantness and I was tough." As editor, she helped structure his work Structuring is a Saturn function. Her Pisces Moon was very sacrificial around the "creative genius." If she wanted to go to New York and Sartre was invited to Yugoslavia, she went with him instead.

As the years pass, transiting and progressed planets will cross the Ascendant and move through your Identify House. *It isn't really empty.* By the time Simone was at the Sorbonne, her progressed Ascendant had entered Sagittarius. When it reached (conjuncted) Sartre's Natal Sagittarian Ascendant degree, he invited her to join his group of friends (she had excelled on the exam that Sartre had failed.) He nicknamed her "Castro" (Beaver) because she studied so hard. After she joined the group, he studied and passed the exam the next time with high marks.

If *no* planets contact the Ascendant degree, it's also possible that your mother remembered your birth time incorrectly (especially when you're part of a large family.) If you haven't a copy of your birth certificate, it's a good idea to obtain one and check the time. If you cannot easily obtain yours (adopted children sometimes have difficulty) it's also a good idea to look for an astrologer who does rectification.

What else influences the astrological Mask besides First House Planets and the spiritual and instinctual planets that rule the Ascendant?

The Elements and the Modes. Let's visualize meeting someone for the first time. A person who might become important to you. Let's say you're at Starbucks to meet an Internet e-mail pal in person; someone from your forum. How do you seem to them? Grounded/Earthy? Imaginative/Watery? Enthusiastic/excited /Firey? Or Aloof, objective/Airy. Air is usually reserved at the first meeting, Though the Airy Mask is friendly, Air is wondering whether they *really* want to get involved. Air is thinking, "He or she might be okay at a distance, I enjoy those e-mails, but do I really want this person any closer than my inbox?"

The Modes (also called Qualities) are influential too: **Cardinality (Aries, Cancer, Libra, Capricorn)** seems authoritative; "together," well organized. The Mask projects: "I have the entire project under control. Let me run through it for you from beginning to end." You'd feel very comfortable having your child or grandchild in his classroom or carpool. Cardinal Masks work well for us when it comes to competition for promotion.

Fixity (Taurus, Leo, Scorpio, Aquarius) has real *presence* but is quite stubborn. Fixity knows who she is; she's sure of herself and quite comfortable in her body. Fixity has the courage of his convictions. He won't be easily persuaded to change his opinions; in fact, he might try to convert you to his religion, philosophy, cause (Aquarius) or political affiliation. (Any Mask, of course, may hide a fragile ego.)

Mutability (Gemini, Virgo, Sagittarius, Pisces) is impressionable, reasonable and maybe even too accommodating (can seem wishy-washy.) They're nice, helpful, impressionable, and suggestible. Like young Professor Mutable. On the first day of class a student wanted to do a term paper on an obscure hobby-topic. The student was very excited about it and Professor Mutable's Mask absorbed the enthusiasm. But the small college library lacked books on the subject, so Professor Mutable brought the student a stack of books he had checked out from a large university library. When the books went missing from the student's locker, Professor Mutable was left with an enormous bill.

It helps if Mutables are in touch with a boundary-setting planet (usually Saturn or Pluto) elsewhere in the chart. Mutable Rising Signs absorb others' energy more than the other Modes, with the exception of Cardinal Water. (Cancer is the psychic-sponge.)

Someone said I have an Intercept. What is that ? How do I work with it?

An entire workshop could be devoted to intercepts! They come up when we use the Tropical Placidus or Tropical Koch formula to calculate horoscopes. By definition, an intercepted Sign is wholly contained within a House but does not appear on a Cusp. People born in the Northern Latitudes are more likely to have them than others.

I don't know whether or not you have planets in your intercept. Intercepted planets usually develop in a solitary way, taking longer to express themselves. There's an excellent book by Joanne Wicklenburg: *Your Hidden Powers, Retrograde Planets and Intercepted Signs.* (American Federation of Astrologers, 1992.) Some people who have intercepted planets are original thinkers; quite imaginative. They seem to have a different perspective on the intercepted House than the rest of us.

As I understand it, I have my Natal Rising Sign for life, though I can also absorb the positive attributes of the Progressed Ascendant as well?

You're right. We came to earth at a certain time and

place. That doesn't change as we progress through the next two or three signs. Let's take an example: Scorpio is a very stubborn (Fixed) Rising Sign. As a child, Scorpio Rising Simone de Beauvoir threw tantrums, or held her breath until she fainted in order to get her own way. It worked for her; her father was absent, her mother at a loss about how to discipline Simone.

As a teenager, she came up against a situation that she couldn't control, even with the Pluto-Ascendant aspect. She wanted to marry her cousin Jacques, who visited often and seemed interested. When she learned that his marriage was already arranged to a wealthy young woman, Simone, who had no dowry, was devastated. She decided never to marry.

Once she progressed into Sagittarius, she found it easier to compromise. With her Fixed Scorpio discipline, she threw herself into her studies at the Sorbonne. She saw philosophy as the key to a "passionate life," the only kind worth living. Influenced by Jean Paul Sartre, whose mind she fell in love with, she renounced the bourgeois values of her upper middle class, conservative Catholic parents for Existentialism and free love. But the mental stimulation was not enough. Her Scorpio libido wanted more.

During the Capricorn progression Beuvoir wrote two novels and her most famous book, *The Second Sex,* without any input from Sartre. Capricorn is the zenith of fame, (symbolically, the Tenth House, the apex house) and she soon had as many fans as Sartre. She was sought as a feminist speaker across America. (The Progressed Ascendant sextiled her Natal Sun and Mercury during this cycle.)

By the time she progressed into Aquarius, Simone lived the "authentic life" she'd longed for as a child. With Chicago author Nelson Algren, she satisfied her Scorpio physical passion and experienced far more than a "marriage of minds!" Though Algren tried to convince her to move to Chicago, she knew Paris was where she belonged. And Algren couldn't accept her relationship with Sartre, with whom she travelled and spent several hours a day.

Her unusual relationship with Sartre included an adult child they had each legally adopted. The two young adopted women sometimes travelled with them; they were an unusual joint family! On Ascendant-square-Ascendant Sartre died; she had a falling-out with his "literary heir."

According to Carl Jung, the *persona* is like an actor's Mask, *but the Mask adapts over time.* In astrology, the progressed 30-year-cycles describe the adaptation.

CAPRICORN RISING

Productive Poet, Scientist, Mentor

Margaret Mead, "I learned the value of hard work by working hard."

—— "Sooner or later I'm going to die, but I'm not going to retire."

—— "The way to do fieldwork is never to come up for air until it is all over."

—— "Even though the ship may go down, the journey goes on."

—— "I must admit that I personally measure success in terms of the contributions an individual makes to her or his fellow human beings."

—— "Old age is like flying through a storm. Once you're aboard, there's nothing you can do."

—— "I was brought up to believe that the only thing worth doing was to add to the sum of accurate information in the world."

Colleen McCullough, "Once I've got the first draft down on paper then I do five or six more drafts, the last two of which will be polishing drafts. The ones in between will flesh out the characters and maybe I'll check my research." Author, *Thorn Birds* and scientist. (neurology)

—— "The lovely thing about being forty is that you can appreciate twenty-five-year-old men more."

James Joyce, "A man's errors are his portals of discovery."

—— "I've put in so many enigmas and puzzles that it will keep the professors busy for centuries arguing over what I meant, and that's the only way of insuring one's immortality." About *Finnegan's Wake.*

—— "Think you're escaping and you'll run into yourself. Longest way round is the shortest way home."

—— "... battles inspired me - not the obvious material battles but those that were fought and won behind your forehead."

—— "When I die, Dublin will be written in my heart."

Marie Curie, "I never see what has been done, I only see what remains to be done."

—— "I was taught that the way of progress is neither swift nor easy."

—— "We must believe that we are gifted for something, and that this thing, at whatever cost, must be attained."

—— "A scientist in his laboratory is not a mere technician: he is also a child confronting natural phenomena that impress him as though they were fairy tales."

—— "You cannot hope to build a better world without improving individuals...each of us must work for his own improvement and at the same time share a general responsibility for all humanity, our particular duty being to aid those to whom we can be most useful."

Albert Einstein, "Marie Curie is, of all celebrated beings, the only one whom fame has not corrupted."

William Butler Yeats, "In dreams begin responsibilities." *Responsibilities.*

—— "Every conquering of temptation represents a new fund of moral energy. Every trial endured and weathered in the right spirit makes a soul nobler and stronger than it was before."

—— "Happiness is neither virtue nor pleasure nor this thing nor that but simply growth. We are happy when we are growing."

Victoria (Vita) Sackville-West, "Growth is exciting; growth is dynamic and alarming. Growth of the soul, growth of the mind." Bloomsbury poet, novelist and world famous horticulturist.

Tennessee Williams, "All of us are guinea pigs in the laboratory of God. Humanity is just a work in progress." Playwright.

—— "Don't look forward to the day you stop suffering, because when it comes you'll know you're dead."

—— "I have always been pushed by the negative. The apparent failure of a play sends me back to my typewriter that very night, before the reviews are out. I am more compelled to get back to work than if I'd had a success."

Joseph Wambaugh, "I enjoy doing the research of nonfiction; that gives me some pleasure, being a detective again." Mystery writer and former policeman.

Dustin Hoffman, "A good review from the critics is just another stay of execution."

Ray Bradbury, "I know you've heard it a thousand times before. But it's true—hard work pays off. If you want to be good, you have to practice, practice, practice. If you don't love something, then don't do it." Novelist, playwright, and producer.

—— "I don't try to describe the future. I try to prevent it." (About his science fiction novels.)

—— "You must stay drunk on writing so reality cannot destroy you."

—— "We are the miracle of force and matter making itself over into imagination and will. Incredible. The Life Force experimenting with forms, You for one, Me for another. The Universe has shouted itself alive. We are the shouts."

—— "The best scientist is open to experience and begins with romance - the idea that anything is possible."

—— "I didn't notice that Maggie was unhappy until she asked me for a divorce in 1957 and again in 1959. I convinced her to stay for the good of the children. In those days, that worked." (About his wife of fifty-seven years.)

Art Buchwald, "I always wanted to get into politics, but I was never light enough to make the team." Critic and columnist.

—— "If you attack the Establishment long enough and hard enough, they'll make you a member of it."

—— "So far, things are going my way. I'm known in the hospice as The Man Who Wouldn't Die."

—— "Whether it's the best of times or the worst of times, it's the only time we've got."

—— "I had a wonderful time celebrating my 80th birthday. My wish was to be 65 again but they—Homeland Security—wouldn't let me."

John Dryden, "Beware the fury of a patient man." English Renaissance author.

—— "Boldness is a mask for fear, however great."

—— "He has not learned the first lesson of life who does not every day surmount a fear."

—— "We first make our habits, and then our habits make us."

—— "Jealousy is the jaundice of the soul."

John Greenleaf Whittier, "For all sad words of tongue and pen/ The saddest are these, 'It might have been.'" Poet ("Snowbound,") novelist and Abolitionist.

—— "The joy that you give to others is the joy that comes back to you."

Candice Bergen, "I got the role I loved the most at a point in my career when most women are being phased out."

—— "I realize I should be grateful that at age 54, people were still offering me film roles. …I've never felt more comfortable in my skin, I've never enjoyed life as much and I feel so lucky. At an age when most actresses are being phased out, I'm being phased in with a vengeance!"

Jane Fonda, "I don't want my wrinkles taken away—I don't want to look like everyone else."

—— "When you can't remember why you're hurt, that's when you're healed."

The Capricorn Mask

I'm the stoic Capricorn Rising Mask. Regardless of the Sun Sign's nature and the Moon Sign's moods, I project responsibility, reliability, and discipline. I make the Sun Sign look well-organized, practical, realistic, and ambitious.

Extremely competitive, I contribute a great deal to my department or organization. I put in the time and effort, I'm no "hanger-on."

I'm the Mask of the CEO; school superintendent, principal, administrator, broker, banker, dean, police commissioner, ambassador, fast food restaurant or property manager. I'm the Mask of politicians who exude *gravitas*; I demand and receive respect. I respect people who live life by the rules; people who also keep their cars washed, their shoes shined and their bills paid on time.

In childhood, parents and teachers consider me mature for my age. Rather than miss an examination or an athletic competition, I'll hide my flu symptoms and go to school. I'm attuned to adults' expectations. Dutiful and diligent, I pitch in whenever I can. Even before I have the vocabulary to express my feelings, I sense adults' anxiety and wish I could alleviate it.

A natural problem-solver, I feel frustrated when too young to help. In youth I usually work very hard, like Margaret Mead and Marie Curie. Like them, I may live on very little while learning my trade, paying my dues and climbing the ladder of success.

Unless, like Tennessee Williams, I have Uranus close to the Rising Sign I'm a traditionalist, cautious and conventional. With Mars (Exalted) near the Ascendant, like Margaret Mead and Jonas Salk, or Mars square it like Ray Bradbury, I'm an explorer who blasts through obstacles and makes discoveries.

Because I identify more with career than other Masks, meaningful work is essential. Like Dustin Hoffman and W.B. Yeats, I believe that a talent—a "gift"—demands a great deal of us and that "talented people cannot be expected to put as much effort into relationships as others."

It's quite possible that I'm an only child, like entrepreneur and oil millionaire John Paul Getty, or the oldest child like Mead and Yeats.

Like Marie Curie, whose father taught science at home, I may assist my father in his work. If I do and I'm a woman, by the time I'm thirty, dad may treat me more like a son than a daughter.

Or, perhaps, like Edward F. ("Teddy") Kennedy, I'm the youngest son. If so, by midlife I may take on responsibility for a parent and/or nieces and nephews as well as my own children. Like Teddy, I may eventually become "the Clan's" Patriarch (or Matriarch.) If I'm the youngest daughter, like journalist Eve Curie, I may live in the shadow of my highly accomplished parents and sibling(s.) Whether my parents are in business; skilled trades, the professions, or the arts and entertainment, like Jane Fonda's, Dustin Hoffman's, and W.B. Yeats,' I learn from them, but family relationships are seldom smooth or easy.

Many who wear my mask follow in their fathers' footsteps. Like Mead, Curie and

Yeats, they identify with, and try to live by, his definition of success.

Unless Venus and/or the Moon are in strong houses (1,4,7, or 10) and/or well-aspected, one or both of my parents is a strict disciplinarian and taskmaster. If both my parents were too busy to spend time with me, I may be closer to a grandparent, like Mead, and Bradbury. If I was a lonely child, I may invent a world of my own, like Irish ex-patriot, James Joyce, who invented his own Dublin.

I love midlife. After forty, I feel much younger than I did in childhood. By fifty, the prime of life, there's no more pressure to add to my resume. There's nothing left to prove to others, *or even to myself.* Though more relaxed and contented, I still want to be productive. Like Hoffman, Bradbury, and Candice Bergen, I still take on interesting projects. Like novelist Alice Walker, I'm still willing to take on difficult topics.

W.B. Yeats was revising his poem, "Under Ben Bulben," the week before he died at seventy-four. Yeats (quoted, above) was right, "we are happiest when we're growing." I'm not content to rest on my laurels.

I like to challenge myself. Self-improvement is no less important in old age than in youth. Less driven now, I still work at improving my tennis backhand or my golf stroke. (If Supreme Court Justice Stevens plays tennis every day at ninety, so can I!)

Some say that mine is a melancholy or

saturnine temperament. *I* think I'm a realist. I do set high standards for myself and, when I fall short of them, I sometimes get depressed.

Like Tennessee Williams with writing (see above,) I learn from my mistakes and my work improves.

Astrologers have called me judgmental, demanding, controlling and even ruthless (while climbing the ladder of success,) but I'm also known for stepping up to the plate in the ninth inning and saving the day when the game is all but lost.

I'm the teacher whose name students remember and whose work ethic they imitate. Whatever my chosen profession, as the poet Longfellow wrote in "Psalm of Life," I'll "leave behind/ Footsteps in the sands of time."

How to Recognize Capricorn Rising

Capricorn Rising can often be recognized by their businesslike manner and their stride. Jeanne Avery, *(The Rising Sign,)* and Joan McEvers (*12 Times 12, 144 Sun/Ascendant Combinations*) both noted Capricorn Rising's tendency to strut. I find this true of shorter Capricorns and horoscopes with the Sun and/or a high percentage of planets in Fire. Capricorn's gait conveys that the boss has arrived and is now in charge; "everything's in order, so let's get started."

Even when they're the job applicant, not the interviewer, Capricorn's firm handshake and serious demeanor sets a businesslike tone. Inwardly, they may be as nervous as the other candidates, especially if they have several planets in Mutability, but the Capricorn Mask projects confidence.

If the interviewer had planned to begin with small talk, once he meets Capricorn Rising, he'll usually change his mind and come right to the point, "this is what the job entails. I've read your resume and you seem a good fit. Tell me how you, as a manager, would develop the department." And having prepared in advance, Capricorn then takes over the interview.

Rarely will Capricorn Rising need a book on dressing for success. They're consummate professionals. Most wear business suits even in hot climates like Florida and Southern California where the dress code is casual and suit jackets are generally reserved for special occasions.

The Capricorn professional favors navy blue, black and gray apparel. One client, a corporate attorney (Libra Sun in the Tenth House) has an extensive collection of colorful shirts and ties to set off his dark suits.

If, however, like Tennessee Williams, Capricorn has Uranus close to the Ascendant degree, he or she will dress more flamboyantly. Artists dress appropriately for their careers, too. Though the artist's apparel may be more colorful than other Capricorns, it's always tasteful, never garish.

For dining out or corporate parties, most Capricorn women choose a little black dress, pearls, and an evening bag full of business cards.

Max Heindel noted in *Message of the Stars* that most have thin, shiny, dark hair which often turns prematurely gray. However, hair color and texture vary with ethnicity; several of my Capricorn Rising clients have curly hair. I've encountered very few blue-eyed blonds with this Ascendant.

Unless Jupiter, Venus or the Moon is in the First House or aspects the Ascendant degree, Capricorn Rising is slender. (Moon/Ascendant indicates a tendency to retain fluids.) Like Margaret Mead, who had Jupiter on her Ascendant, Capricorn may become overextended and "too busy to exercise." He or she tends to gain weight at midife, especially during the Jupiter Return years, (36, 48, 60, and 72) unless Saturn's house position and aspects offset Jupiter's.

Mead, the Earth Mother, seemed comfortable with her weight. Actress Jane Fonda, on the other hand, struggled for twenty-three years with bulimia. Her Capricorn perfectionism fought a tendency to be rotund. (Jupiter-in-Fall in the First House.)

Jupiter, the Moon and Venus in, or aspecting, the First House indicate a warm, nurturing Mask. If Jupiter is stronger by house position than Saturn, (1,4, 7,or 10) Capricorn's cup of Life seems half full. If Saturn is stronger, Capricorn sees the cup as half empty. With Saturn-in-the-First or aspecting the Ascendant degree, the Mask is cool, distant, and may seem judgmental.

Though the horoscope may be shy or sensitive, this Mask hides fear, anxiety and insecurity well. Like a suit of armor, it provides a strong defense. It's also the Zodiac's best boundary-setter.

Heindel observed that Capricorn Rising people have thin necks. I find this is true until their forties or early fifties.

In Heindel's experience, Capricorn is a short Rising Sign. At five feet tall, Margaret Mead is an example. My own experience, however, has been more like Jeanne Avery's. She found that some Capricorn Rising people are tall with large feet and hands, like Sean Connery. A few are knock-kneed. But there are also many short Capricorns with small wrists, ankles, hands and feet. Both tall, rangy, Capricorns and shorter ones tend towards osteoarthritis or osteoporosis as they grow older.

Even Jane Fonda, known as "Queen of the Workout" after her famous exercise video, had a hip and knee replacement in her late sixties.[1] These are fairly common surgeries for Capricorn Sun and Ascendant.

After fifty, Capricorn Rising tends to stoop, as if the weight of the world is pressing down on their shoulders. Yoga stretches for both the upper and lower back are highly recommended.

This Rising Sign can also be recognized by its wry sense of humor, which resembles Scorpio's but isn't quite as dark. Capricorn humor is often self-deprecating. Some examples are Dustin Hoffman's performance as Benjamin in *The Graduate,* Alan Alda's as Hawkeye in *Mash* and in Jane Fonda in *Barbarella*[2]

1 "Body Talk," Deborah Soloman's interview with Jane Fonda, now 72 years old, in the *New York Times Magazine,* April 19, 2010. Fonda's original exercise video sold the most copies. She believes it started a trend.

2 directed by her first husband Roger Vadim.

though all three actors are remembered for their more serious roles.

Art Buchwald wrote satirical columns and speeches. He once gave a commencement address at Tulane University, wishing the graduating attorneys success in "defending those poor, unfortunate banks and corporations from the widows and orphans who persecute them." English Renaissance poet John Dryden was famous for his satirical couplets.

Ray Bradbury used sardonic humor against censorship, particularly book burning, in *Fahrenheit 451.* (The title derives from the temperature at which paper burns.) The anthology's short stories were first published during Senator Joseph McCarthy's Un-American Activities Committee hearings.[3]

Many highly-disciplined self-made men and women have this Ascendant. Successful artists, writers and entrepreneurs often mention strict parents who praised hard work and achievement but were not affectionate.

Several clients lost their mothers in childhood, as did Marie Sklowdowska (Curie,) Jane Fonda, and Art Buchwald.

An autodidact whose post-secondary education "consisted of ten years at the public library," Ray Bradbury joked that his mother, Esther, was "a stoic Swedish lady of the Victorian generation," and that "her girdle must have been too tight."

3 This and other references to Ray Douglas Bradbury are taken from Sam Weller's *The Bradbury Chronicles: The Life of Ray Bradbury, Predicting the Past, Remembering the Future*, (NY: HarperCollins,) 2005.

Before Ray was born, she'd lost one of her twin sons, Sam, to influenza. So, whenever little Ray played in the yard, Esther worried. She attached him to a tree by a long rope. But she took him to the movie theater every afternoon; it was cooler than the house in summer and warmer in wintertime. When Ray's infant sister died, he never saw Esther weep.

During the Depression, the family was very poor. His father moved them West twice, attempting to find work; then moved them back to Waukegan, Illinois.[4] Wherever they lived, until their late teens, Ray and his older brother Skip shared a sofa bed. Yet, his was one of the *happiest* Capricorn Rising childhoods in this chapter. He often looked back nostalgically at his early years in Illinois and some of his best work was set in the Midwest.

By midlife, some Capricorns come to understand their parents' inability to nurture. They realize that because one or both their parents may have lacked nurturing as children, their parent or parents were unable to provide it to their own children. It may take a long time, though, for Capricorn to move beyond intellectual understanding to forgiveness.

More often than other Rising Signs, Capricorn clients will volunteer information about their early childhood and/or mention their birth order in the family. (Their siblings, though raised by the same parents, seldom do so.)

---

4 The third attempt, when Ray was thirteen, succeeded partly because other relatives were established in Los Angeles by then to help the family settle. Ray was happier once his grandmother and Aunt Neva joined them.

Like Eve Curie (see above, "The Mask") they're usually quite accomplished, yet they'll often compare their success to others' in a self-deprecatory way. Jane Fonda, who received two Oscars and many nominations, is an example of Capricorn's tendency to keep proving themselves.[5]

Poet and playwright William Butler Yeats was an autodidact, like Ray Bradbury. Yeats' younger brother, Jack followed in their father's footsteps and became a painter. By choosing literature, young "Willie" differentiated himself from them and their aesthetic

5 See Jane Fonda, *My Life So Far,* (NY: Random House) 2005. Adult Capricorn Rising clients often mention a parent who was physically or emotionally absent. Fonda's mother was hospitalized with mental problems; she killed herself when Jane was 13. Curie's mother died when she was ten. While researching her dissertation, Mead's mother took little Margaret along on her interviews. After the death of her infant sister, Katherine, Mead's father withdrew emotionally to avoid the pain of attachment and loss. Mead mothered her younger sisters and wrote plays to showcase their talents. She addressed her letters from Samoa to her grandmother, who'd always found time for her. Art Buchwald's father placed him in a Jewish orphanage, then confused him by visiting for two years. Art developed his sardonic humor in foster homes. He considered the Marines his first real family. Bradbury seemed closer to his grandparents and "creative" Aunt Neva than his parents. The last few years of his father's life, the two bonded.

standards. He avoided any odious comparisons they might have made about his work.[6]

Eve Curie, daughter of scientist Marie Curie, had Mercury and Uranus conjunct her Ascendant. She chose journalism and public speaking over science, the family career.[7]

Astrologers associate Capricorn Rising with the survival instinct and longevity. Those who find fulfilling work seem happiest. They expect to live to a ripe old age. Like CNN host, Larry King and the examples in the quoted above, Capricorn Rising people who love their work seldom intend to retire. They remain productive well into old age.

The Mundane Ruler - Saturn

"Striving, ever striving! At last, behold the goal!"
Parmahansa Yogananda

In astrology and alchemy, Saturn's mineral is lead.

---

6 Later, the father, John B. Yeats, distanced himself from the son by moving to New York, ostensibly to paint portraits for the wealthy. Instead, he enjoyed lecturing at the YMCA for small fees. "Willie" Yeats paid his father's bills whenever he passed through the city to lecture or read poetry. Distance seemed to improve their relationship; the father began to express his pride in and admiration for his son to others.

7 *Astrodienst* (www. astro.com) has a horoscope for her older sister Irene (9/12/1897) with Gemini Rising. I was unable to find an accurate horoscope for her father, Pierre, who died while Eve was very young.

Saturn endures. In Saturn's Natal House, regardless of our Rising Sign, we're rooted, grounded, and weighed down. Many challenges come to Capricorn in Saturn's Natal House, as well as in House Ten (career.) In youth, Capricorn learns to set boundaries and build defenses. Over the years, their armor grows thicker, like the scales of the mythical crocodile, Makara, a Capricorn symbol.[8]

A well aspected Saturn helps with timing—success may not take as long—but a badly aspected Saturn may result in the feeling that Capricorn is working very hard just to stay in the same place. But if, as Yogananda (Sun-in-Capricorn) recommended, they "keep on keeping on," they'll eventually succeed. (Saturn is the symbol for Father Time.) With Saturnine discipline and focus, they achieve their goals.

The secret to working with the mundane ruler seems to be, *don't struggle in Saturn's House.* Once Capricorn Rising relaxes about his desires, leaves room in his life and opens his heart, grace intervenes. Once his heart is open, he becomes more Yin. As Capricorns release their expectations and preconceptions, they become more receptive to Life; their timing improves.

But also important to let go of thoughts like, "I don't need any help, *I can make this happen by myself.*" And,

8 See Alice A. Bailey, *Esoteric Astrology,* (NY: Lucis,) 1972, "Capricorn" on the three symbols for the three stages of Capricorn, the Goat, the Crocodile, and the Unicorn. Makara was the vehicle on which the Vedic god Varuna, who controlled the changing seasons, traveled. The same armor that may have been necessary for survival in youth becomes brittle after fifty. It's hard to live by Saturn's shoulds and oughts.

"I have to do it perfectly." This becomes easier with the aid of a spiritual technique such as meditation, yoga, or journal writing; anything that increases self-awareness and offers "time-out" from the thoughts circling through his mind.

One day, Capricorn will observe that he's beginning to attract different, more congenial people. Or, he'll find that he appreciates the people who're *already* in his life and the success he's *already* achieved. He'll stop waiting for the perfect job or the perfect mate to appear on the doorstep.

Saturn also represents long-term planning. Margaret Mead chose her three husbands carefully, each for a different reason. With Jupiter on her Ascendant, she drew interesting men and generously helped get them grants. She nurtured their careers. But when Ruth Benedict, her friend and lover of thirty years died, Mead suddenly realized what the relationship had meant to her. She fell apart emotionally.

"I read everything she ever wrote; she read everything I've ever written. Neither of us could say that about anyone else," she wrote in her autobiography, *Blackberry Winter.* Her daughter, Catherine Bateson, wrote that though she'd known the two women were friends, her mother had *many* women friends. She was unable to understand Margaret's loss or the depth of her sorrow over Ruth.

Margaret and Ruth had kept quiet about their relationship. Capricorn Rising sacrifices a great deal for career. Because the Tenth Sign is analogous to the Tenth House, Capricorn is invested in success.

The Saturn Chakra is associated with anxiety, fear and self-doubt, those "Saturn worries" like, "what will people think of me? What will happen to my career if people find out about Ruth and me?"

The most common Saturn worries are failure in career; poor health, premature death, and fear of financial loss or outliving their money.

As they grow older, Capricorn men often remark, "one of my parents developed a certain illness at 58; *I'll* soon be 58! Will *I* be diagnosed with it?" The more he worries, the more certain Capricorn becomes that he has the parent's DNA and all the symptoms! Yoga, which works with the breath to release fear, anxiety and stress, can be really helpful.[9]

Finally, Saturn is associated with Father and male relatives. If Saturn is not well-aspected, Capricorn Rising's relationship with his or her father can be difficult.

Though it's usually Capricorn Rising, not the parent, who moves cross-country, Capricorn often comments, as Yeats did, on "the freedom that distance allows" in relating to "a difficult" parent.[10]

---

9 Poses like the pigeon and downward facing dog are recommended.

10 Yeats and his father became congenial correspondents. J.B. no longer knew about his son's important decisions until after they'd been made and carried out.

The Moon-Saturn Balance
Dreams, Imagination, the Writing process, Sensitivity, Nurturing, Support

Lunar Imagination is a powerful antidote to Saturn fears; it enables us to see beyond them. Imagination belongs to our Feminine, lunar nature. Integrating the lunar side is also important to balanced living. For Capricorn Rising, it's symbolized by Moon-ruled Cancer, the Sign located opposite the Ascendant, on the Seventh House cusp. (Marriage and other one-on-one relationships.) Whether in dreams or waking-state awareness, it's important to face our fears and find a way to transcend them.[11]

Prior to America's entry into World War II, Ray Bradbury dreamed of being chased by a large, black bulldog. The dog eventually caught and ate him; Bradbury died in the dream. He awoke terrified! He knew at once what it meant. In the coming war, his life would be cut off like that of his talented young uncle in World War I. Like his uncle, he'd never have an opportunity to realize his talents. He sat up in bed and said aloud, "I'm going to *live* for my country."[12]

He need not have worried. By the time World War II

---

11 John Dryden (see above quote) and W.B. Yeats, in his *Memoirs,* both wrote about conquering fear.

12 A classmate told Bradbury's biographer that Ray wore the suit in which his uncle was shot under his graduation gown and showed classmates the bullet hole. Whether or not the anecdote is true, it's clear the story of the uncle's death left a strong impression on Ray. His classmate remembered it.

was declared, Ray's eyesight was so poor that he failed the army physical. And, in a sense, he did "live for his country." Through his imagination, Bradbury created a mythology for the Space Age. He wrote of aliens, rocket ships to Mars, and astronauts for whom space travel was as commonplace as driving a truck cross-country. He helped prepare a generation for what lay ahead. In the 1930's and 40's, he foresaw televisions hanging on walls and many electronic devices that were invented decades later.

Though Capricorn is the polar opposite of Cancer Rising, (the former is stoic and pragmatic; the latter feeling-oriented, often hypersensitive) both Signs have long memories and face similar issues around letting go of childhood misunderstandings and resentments.

Many adults still hurt from past wounds, from being victimized when they were too young to fight back against powerful adults. Anger and frustration are usually directed at parents, though like James Joyce and the Jesuits, sometimes these emotions are directed at teachers.[13]

Jane Fonda put it well when she said, "*when you can't remember why you're hurt, that's when you're healed.*"

Capricorn Rising, people of both sexes seek nurturing (the Cancer Archetype) in marriage. Margaret Mead loved her first husband, divinity student Luther Cressman, for his sensitivity; he was so unlike her father! He joined the Episcopal Church

13 Joyce later made his peace with his former teachers, admitting that without them he might have been a sloppy thinker.

as she suggested, but a few years later he found that he lacked a religious vocation. For Mead, the marriage seemed to lose its purpose; as she would no longer be a minister's wife.[14]

Later, when Mead discovered she could conceive a child,[15] she chose her third husband, Gregory Bateson, in the belief that he'd be a more nurturing parent than Reo Fortune, her second husband and fieldwork companion.

Though pragmatic about her choices, sensitivity and emotional support mattered to Margaret. Her First House Moon was a powerful influence. (Her First House Venus, another feminine planet, added warmth to the Mask.)

However, with Mars and Saturn on the Ascendant, she also valued masculine strength. When they met on shipboard, Reo Fortune was finishing his degree in psychology. By the end of the voyage, he'd decided to prepare for Margaret's field, anthropology. More macho than her first husband, Mead thought the young New Zealander would be a good companion in remote villages, some of whose inhabitants were one generation removed from cannibalism.[16]

14 Jane Howard, *Margaret Mead: A Life,* (NY: Ballantine,) 1984, 36. They were engaged five years, followed by what both later called their "student marriage." They lived in New York, then she left for Samoa and he left for London and Paris. Cressman eventually became an archeologist.

15 Because her uterus was tipped, a doctor told her it was unlikely she could become pregnant. After miscarrying twice in the field, she decided the doctor was wrong.

16 They were in New Guinea and the Admiralty Islands together.

With Saturn-in-Rulership, Mars-in-Exaltation, and Jupiter-in-Fall lined up on her Ascendant, ages thirty and sixty, the Saturn and Jupiter years, were milestones in Margaret's life.

Exalted Mars played its role. She spoke of giving students and others "a transfusion of extra energy," which they appreciated when working "at the top of their capacity, but seemed to resent when they weren't."[17]Gregory Bateson had considered suicide shortly before meeting Margaret. Her enthusiasm for his theories changed his mind. They fell in love doing fieldwork along the Sepik River, while Mead was still married to Fortune.

Jane Fonda, too, valued sensitivity in a husband. She found it in Tom Hayden, her second husband, who was gentle and respectful with her daughter, Vanessa. Both Fonda and Mead had very strict fathers and chose disciplined, ambitious husbands.

My women clients tend to follow the same pattern. However, a husband who goes beyond ambitious to *driven* will soon seem "too much like dad." Cancer on the Seventh House symbolizes a creative spouse, a spouse more sensitive than Dad. Yet, Natal Saturn appreciates ambition in a man!

Capricorn Rising men often choose an Earth Mother type, a woman like James Joyce's Nora Barnacle, the prototype for Molly Bloom in his novel, *Ulysses*. Their

---

17 *Blackberry Winter,* cited above, 181. Many of us with Mars close to our Ascendant have had similar experiences with the "energy transfusion, though Mars-in-Exaltation has a particularly strong impact.

grandson, Steven, said that without Nora, Joyce "could not have written one book!"[18]

William Butler Yeats, who, like Mead had a First House Moon-in-Detriment, married Georgia Hyde Lees at fifty-one. She brought him the gift of automatic handwriting, a new source of metaphor. He gave up séances and mediums; he'd "found peace and harmony." When Georgia became seriously ill with influenza in 1918, Yeats' father wrote a friend that if she died, "Willie would fall to pieces."[19] His biographer Richard Ellmann believed that without her, Yeats would have been considered a minor poet.

Earth Mothers endure. Though her husband called her "the family intellectual,"[20] Marguerite McClure Bradbury was a supportive wife and devoted mother of four. Like Nora Joyce, the Earth Mother is often the stronger personality in the marriage. While James

---

18 Brenda Maddox, *Nora: The Real Life of Molly Bloom,* (Boston: Houghton-Mifflin,) 1988. Steven's quote, 376. Joyce and Nora were together thirty-seven years, until his death from peritonitis. Like so many Capricorn Rising stoics, he diagnosed himself instead of visiting a doctor. He was certain he had stomach cancer. His ulcer was treatable in the early stages but became perforated.

19 Richard Ellmann, *Yeats: the Man and the Masks,* (London: W.W. Norton) 1979,114 and preface, ix.

20 Maggie said that marriage to Ray was like taking a vow of poverty. She spoke four languages and was re-reading Proust in French when Sam Weller, Ray's biographer, met her. She attended UCLA; she loved Proust and Yeats. Her husband was self-taught; he loved Buck Rogers comic strips, science fiction and fantasy novels. He wrote for the Alfred Hitchcock Show and the Twilight Zone.

Joyce was vociferously anti-Catholic, Nora raised their two children and their grandson as Catholics.

Mead became anthropology's matriarch. (She was also called its "evangelist" for her recruiting efforts.)[21]

In summary, the Moon, ruler of the Seventh House for Capricorn Rising, represents the feminine, Mother, women relatives, feelings, intuition and imagination. Saturn, the mundane ruler, represents the masculine, Father, male relatives; focus, discipline, pragmatism, rationality. Even when Capricorn Rising has a prominent First House Moon like Mead and Yeats, it's quite a challenge to integrate Saturn and the Moon within.[22]

The Cancer Rising Chapter in *Beyond the Mask, Part I*, on William Blake, (the Creative Imagination

21 She once remarked at a conference, "we (anthropologists) are a family and we will not have differences of opinion before strangers.

22 However, it can be magical when the two planets— or the masculine and feminine sides—unite to create a literary work! Bradbury combined his sensate powers of observation with the lunar gift for metaphor. One evening he and his wife were walking on the beach near Venice pier, where the city had let nature reclaim an amusement park. The rollercoaster lay on its side in the sand. "Look! The bones of a dinosaur," Ray said to Maggie, pointing to it. Then, suddenly, a foghorn blew and the metaphor became a story. "The dinosaur's mate is calling to it from the depths of the ocean!" And later, as the story developed, a dinosaur heard the foghorn, awoke after millions of years and emerged from the sea in search of its lost mate. But the sight of the skeleton on the beach infuriated him! The dinosaur charged the lighthouse, the source of the foghorn sound.

theme,) and Christopher Isherwood, (on memoirs and the Writing Cure) might be interesting if you have Cancer on your Seventh House cusp. Memoir writing can be a healing process for both Cancer and Capricorn Rising. Both Signs have very long memories.

Eve Curie, with Capricorn Rising, also wrote a memoir.[23] Because Eve was only two years old when her father, Pierre, died, her sister's recollections filled many gaps in her memories. During the writing process, Eve came to understand her mother's close relationship with her older sister, Irene. Marie and Irene had gone to the lab together every day, leaving little Eve with a sitter. Irene eventually married Marie's most trusted lab assistant. Later, after Marie's death, the couple took over the Curies' work.

Catherine Bateson, the only child of Margaret Mead and Gregory Bateson, wrote an engaging memoir about her parents and her childhood. Her parents believed early childhood development was crucial, so they "found her an excellent English nanny." They once spent "an entire weekend" caring for little Cathy themselves "to see what it was like," but apparently they didn't repeat the experience![24]

23 *Madame Curie: A Biography by Eve Curie,* Vincent Sheean trans, (NY: Doubleday,) 1938.

24 In fairness to Mead and Gregory Bateson, they were both occupied with the war effort at the time. The British government loaned Bateson, who was OSS, to Washington. After Pearl Harbor, the American government put his knowledge of the Pacific to use. Margaret moved to Washington DC and also involved in classified projects around her teaching schedule and her work at the Natural History Museum.

The Moon and Intuition

Mead's "complex empathy and imagination," according to her daughter, was "capable of seeing possible futures" for others, futures that "eluded them." As a child, she'd seen her mother hurt when others called her domineering, so, at thirteen, Catherine decided to avoid a later quarrel with Margaret and future pain. She convinced Margaret to let her stay in Israel and learn Middle Eastern languages. She decided to find her own way lest her future, too, be set in motion by Margaret's "daydreams." If she became a linguist, not an anthropologist, neither parent would know the languages or the region in which she specialized. As an adult, Catherine considered that a pivotal decision in her life.[25]

Later, however, she became an anthropologist. When, after her mother's death, Bateson interviewed Mead's first and second husbands, her research validated her childhood impressions. They'd both come to resent Margaret's "complex empathy."

It helps if Capricorn Rising had a childhood influence who encouraged him or her to develop their intuition and imagination. Ray Bradbury had his granny, his "artistic Aunt Neva" and encouraging teachers.

Margaret Mead's grandmother assured her that a woman "could have it all," a fulfilling career and

25 Catherine Bateson, *With a Daughter's Eye: A Memoir of Margaret Mead and Gregory Bateson,* (NY: HarperCollins Perennial,) 1984, *passim.* Looking back on her decision at 13, it later seemed critical to her life development.

motherhood. Mead wrote poetry in college. Her prose style, devoid of social science jargon, reached mainstream America through *Redbook* magazine.

William B. Yeats developed his lunar, imaginative side as a child in his mother's kitchen in Sligo, Ireland, listening to stories of ghosts and fairies. Though an imaginative artist, WBY's father, John B. Yeats, preferred the Utilitarian philosophy. Father and son argued vehemently about that and other subjects. Once, in the course of an argument about John Ruskin, J.B. Yeats pushed young Willie against a wall so hard that he "broke the glass on a picture with the back of my head."[26]

His mother's folk stories nourished one side of the poet's Gemini (Sun Sign) personality; his father's skeptical philosophy influenced the other.

Later as an adult, the symbol of the two rotating gyres, (which came from the automatic writing,) seemed to help Yeats in reconciling the Gemini opposites. Writing and revising *A Vision* helped him reconcile his public and private personalities, especially the dialogue between the skeptical politician, "Owen Aherne," and the more mystical "Michael Robartes."[27]

The third symbol for Capricorn is the beautiful,

26 Ellmann, cited above, 278. His sister told a friend that the house was much quieter "after Willie got his own place, without WIllie and father constantly shouting at each other." Their father had the children make up stories to develop their narrative skills. "How was today's trip to the mailbox different from yesterday's?" He taught them that the arts were as important as the sciences.

27 There is a sketch of the gyres in *A Vision.* (Gyres is pronounced with a hard "g.")

pure white Unicorn with big blue eyes. In folklore, he stares into the Abyss of materialism.

Sure-footed, he stands at the edge of the pit and shines his horn, "the light of discrimination," downward, dispelling fear of death and the illusion of insufficiency. Alice Bailey tells us that "when the goat becomes the Unicorn, he "no longer wanders arid paths in fear of his unknown future."[28]

The Esoteric Ruler - Saturn as Dharma Higher Self and Selfless Service - The Fearless Unicorn Gazes at the Stars

Saturn rules Capricorn at two different levels; the mundane, where the plucky, sure-footed mountain goat ascends to the pinnacle of material success at the Zenith of the horoscope,[29] and the esoteric, where the rare, fleet-footed Unicorn, a symbol of the Self, may appear in dreams or call out to Capricorn in some

---

28 Scorpio Rising Friedrich Nietzsche warns not to stare too long into the Abyss, lest it stare back at us. See also Alice A. Bailey, cited above, "Capricorn," (NY: Lucis Press) 1972. The single horn symbolizes single-pointed concentration. The Unicorn's horn is located at its "third eye." Associated with the pineal gland, the third eye is said to control the endocrine system in esoteric healing.

29 The Zenith is the cusp of the Tenth House, analogous to the Tenth Sign, Capricorn. In numerology, the Number Ten is reduced to One, the number of Wholeness, by adding the digits, One and Zero.

other way. Carl Jung associated the Unicorn with the alchemical *Spiritus Mercurius.*

Though most of us are familiar with the gentle Unicorn tamed by the innocent young girl,[30] Unicorns are also fierce. A client, chased by a unicorn in a dream, told me it felt like being pursued by the 'Hound of Heaven' in Francis Thompson's poem:

> I fled Him, down the nights and down the days/ I fled Him, down the arches of the years/ I fled Him, down the labyrinthine ways/ Of my own mind; and in the mist of tears/ I hid from Him/ and under running laughter/ Up vistaed hopes I sped/ And shot, precipitated, /down Titanic glooms of chasmèd fears/ From those strong Feet that followed, followed after/ But with unhurrying chase, And unperturbéd pace/ Deliberate speed, majestic instancy, They beat—and a Voice beat/More instant than the Feet—/"All things betray thee, who betrayest Me."

She interpreted the dream's message as, "he'll run me through with his sharp horn if I don't start paying attention to Psyche around my busy schedule!"

According to biographer Virginia Moore,[31] W.B.

30 "La Dame a la Licorne" is on a series of 15th Century Belgian tapestries, representing the five senses. They're in the Musee de Cluny in Paris. Gentle and compassionate Quan Yin has a small, spotted unicorn. In Chinese folklore, the unicorn is the noblest of animals and said to live 1,000 years.

31 Virginia Moore, *The Unicorn: W.B. Yeats' Search for Reality,* (NY: Macmillan,) 1954.

Yeats was captivated by a painting of two unicorns in side-by-side panels. One stands next to a Victorian maiden wearing an elaborate brocade dress, while the other, more libidinous unicorn,[32] has his head in a naked woman's lap. Yeats supposedly contemplated this painting for a long time. He chose the Unicorn as the symbol for his third initiation in the Golden Dawn Society, and took the name, *Monoceris de astris,* "Unicorn from the Stars."[33]

While fascinated with the symbol, Yeats wrote two plays, "The Unicorn from the Stars" and, (with his patroness, Lady Gregory,) "Where There is Nothing, There is God."[34] Reviewers and theater audiences alike were *un*impressed. Their verdict was that though symbolism "may enrich poetry and plays, it's a poor substitute for a plot." Yet, these plays were Yeats' personal favorites. He felt they belonged in the "canon" of his works.

What's it like when Capricorn removes his armor

---

32 Unicorn horn was considered an aphrodisiac during the Middle Ages; hunters hoped to trap them, using maidens as bait. It was also considered a magical cure for many ills and the antidote to poison.

33 Yeats wrote to his sister Elizabeth, "most people don't know that the Unicorn is a symbol of the soul. It's a personal symbol for me as it's the name of my grade level—level three-in the Golden Dawn. See Kathleen Worth, "Where There Is Nothing, There is God," (Washington DC: Catholic University of America Press,) 1987. Worth also states that the Paul character is modeled on his father, J.B. Yeats, "full of a hard passion and a mad reverie," according to his son. See her introduction.

34 "Where There is Nothing, There Is God," cited above.

(defenses) at the end of the crocodile phase and leaves the arid path of materialism to follow the way of the Unicorn? Or, for that matter, what's it like for *any of us to* relax and make our peace with Saturn? We leave behind self-doubt; financial insecurity, fear of failure as professionals, scientists, writers or artists. Capricorn Rising also transcends the fear of being forgotten (not living on in others' memories, a type of immortality) and the fear of death.

Yeats once wrote of a fear that "this alchemist had been working for a long time with the wrong *prima materia.*" That fear, too, had disappeared.

The Unicorn is fearless! As he gazing at the stars *(asters,)* he glimpses eternity.

Ray Bradbury wanted to be famous; his Leo Sun Sign's agenda and Capricorn Mask worked well together. As a young man, he tried acting first. Later, he hoped to be remembered like his heroes, science fiction and fantasy authors, H.G. Wells, Robert A. Heinlein, and Edgar Rice Burroughs. He kept on writing short stories. By midlife, he was happily surprised to discover that he was considered a mainstream author.

James Joyce sought to carve himself a niche in literature unoccupied by any other famous Irish writer. GB Shaw and JM Synge were the playwrights and Yeats the famous Irish poet, so young Joyce decided to become a novelist. He developed his "stream-of-consciousness" narrative style in *Ulysses*; the rhythm was similar to his wife Nora's Galway speech patterns.[35]

In the 1950's and early 60's, many American teachers encouraged students to imitate the stream-of-consciousness technique. Joyce also employed symbolism as a literary gimmick, "hoping to keep literature professors busy for three hundred years figuring out *Finnegan's Wake*."

Yeats extolled his readers, future generations of "Irishry," to learn their craft well, polish their lines and live up to the standards of those who went before.[36] For Yeats and Joyce, literary immortality involved a great deal of effort.

But Capricorn's high standards aren't limited to the literary arts, the social sciences, or Madame Curie's lab. Actress Jane Fonda improved her performance with each movie. She won two Oscars; several of her films have become classics. Art Buchwald won a Pulitzer; Marie Curie and Yeats won Nobel Prizes.

Margaret Mead became a household word and received the Congressional Medal of Freedom posthumously. Although she wasn't offered a cabinet post, Margaret achieved all her other goals. She's

---

35 His characters repeated the same phrase twice, as Galway people did, like, "I pray every day. I pray every day for rain," and often began conversations with the phrase, "do you think…?"

36 "Under Ben Bulben," V, "Irish poets, learn your trade/ Sing whatever is well made./that we in coming days may be/Still the indomitable Irishry." *Collected Poems,* 327.

had her share of detractors but her work lives on.[37] Mountain goats do reach those lofty Tenth House peaks! Many students of my generation changed their majors to anthropology because of Mead's sense of urgency about documenting vanishing languages and "pre-industrial cultures."[38]

Yeats defined happiness as personal growth. "We're happiest when we're growing." (See above list of quotes.) To esoteric Capricorns, growth is more important than achievement.

As Paramahansa Yogananda (Sun-in- Capricorn) once said, "we don't want to become psychological antiques." Between forty and fifty, many mountain goats move beyond self-doubt and the need for approval, which comes across to others as defensiveness. They've come to realize that they, themselves, *are* the *prima materia.*

Margaret Mead loved to write poetry but gave it up

---

37 A colleague once called her a "lady novelist." Because her first book, *Coming of Age in Samoa* was so well-written, it was read by many outside anthropology. A First House Moon may indicate that the general public will identify with the author's work.

38 As a graduate student, Mead once woke up thinking that the last old man on Rarotonga might die *that day,* before she had a chance to interview him! As it turned out, she worked mainly with women and children.

"after his (Bateson's) criticism killed the impulse."[39] But she didn't give up writing! Her clear, simple, direct style reached a wide audience through *Redbook.*

In *My Life So Far,* Fonda looked back on bulimia and breast implants in wonderment and asked herself, "why did I care so much what others thought of me? Why did their approval seem so important?" Unlike most actresses, Fonda made peace with her "character lines," or wrinkles.

Breakthroughs occur at every level, emotional, spiritual and physical. After Yeats reconciled with his lost love, Maud Gonne, and they became "spiritual friends," he wrote, "When day begins to break/I count my good and bad/Being wakeful for her sake/ Remembering what she had/What eagle look still shows/*While up from my heart's root/So great a sweetness flows/ I shake from head to foot.*"

Jupiter is the antidote to Saturn' s work obsession. As the principle of limitation, Saturn excels at focus, discipline and boundary-setting. But when carried to extremes, Saturn's dedication to career results in unbalanced living. As the principle of expansion, Jupiter opens wide the door of experience to those Capricorns willing to take risks.

As long as Ray Bradbury, who had a Sagittarian (Jupiter-ruled) Moon, sadly affirmed, "I'll *never*

---

39 *With a Daughter's Eye,* cited above, 42. She did write a beautiful poem for her daughter, untitled. It's in her memoir, *Blackberry Winter.* Cited above, pp 271-72. With the kind permission of the Institute for Intercultural Studies, I once read it at a Mother's Day workshop. Participants really enjoyed it.

have enough money to travel to Europe," he limited himself. However, after he agreed to collaborate with John Huston, the world opened to him. He spent six months in Ireland, then visited other countries. Still, it wasn't easy. His phobias about flying and driving still restricted him.[40] He missed American hamburgers and other familiar food.

There's a Kafka short story about a mouse who lived in a wall which illustrates Saturn's narrowness as the Principle of Limitation. In this story, the mouse felt safe only in small spaces; he avoided the wide passages as he navigated his maze. Then, one day, moving along with his flanks securely pressed against the narrow passage, he saw light at the end of his tunnel.

However, as he came to the last stage of his journey to freedom, he saw a mousetrap blocking the exit. He stopped to stare at it, wondering, "what now?" Then he heard a sonorous voice say, "*you can do this,* you're almost out! I'll guide you; just back up a bit away from the trap and move slightly to the right, between the trap and the wall."

The frightened mouse did as suggested, edging himself slowly towards the right of the exit hole. Suddenly, a paw reached in and snagged him; the sonorous voice belonged to a purring cat! It's not wise to act in fear.

---

40 I suspect his Moon was in the Twelfth, not the Eleventh, because the Twelfth, (opposite the Sixth,) is, in my experience, the more likely position for phobias. John Huston threatened to leave him in Ireland unless Bradbury would fly to England with him but Ray took a boat and met him there.

Like Scorpio, Capricorn Rising works well in solitude. However, it's possible to take austerity to extremes. During her student years at the Sorbonne, Marie Curie's sister and brother-in-law would have welcomed her into their comfortable Paris home. Marie, after all, had worked as a governess in Poland to pay for her sister's training.

Instead, Marie rented an attic apartment that was freezing cold in winter and insufferably hot in summer. When she fainted and was diagnosed with pneumonia and malnutrition, her sister insisted she come to live with them. But as soon as she recovered, Marie returned to the garret.

Even after she married Pierre, an older scientist with a salary from the Sorbonne, the couple lived austerely. Her vacations involved hiking in the mountains while discussing physics with her husband or Albert Einstein, when he joined them. Her mind was always on her work, and *it was never finished.* (See the list of quotes, above.)

As Assistant Curator, Margaret Mead enjoyed her solitude in her aerie on the top floor of the Museum of Natural History. She seldom went to lunch with her peers. A colleague once tracked her to her lair, remarking, "the staff downstairs weren't sure if you were even in the country. They haven't seen you in months; they thought perhaps you were off doing field- work." Mead smiled and told him she liked it that away; she accomplished so much more when everyone thought she was away.

Mead risked her health for her career. When

her thesis advisor wanted her to work with Native Americans, Margaret insisted on the Pacific Islanders instead. Even after her return to the United States, Mead suffered from bouts of malaria. She needed quinine immediately after giving birth to her daughter. Curie's mysterious symptoms prior to her death are attributed by many biographers to working with radioactive elements without any protection, even gloves. (At the time, scientists didn't know protection was necessary.)

Solitude needn't mean privation. In contrast to Saturn, Jupiter is generous; Capricorns with a prominent or well-aspected Jupiter are generous *with themselves* as well as others. Esoteric Capricorns are known for generosity with their time and resources. Saturn may still whisper, "you shouldn't buy that; you'd better not take that trip! You might outlive your money," but Jupiter represents faith in Life, and in abundance.

Even if Jupiter is stronger by house and aspect than Saturn, Capricorn Rising is seldom extravagant. He or she *is,* however, more likely to believe that "God will provide" at the end of life; and all basic needs will be met.

Mead, with her widespread friends and acquaintances, experienced the world as a global village. With a prominent Jupiter, Capricorn Rising is often enriched by relationships with gifted and interesting people.

Capricorns who slow down and take an occasional

sometimes be harmful? Astrologers are often asked by Capricorn parents why a child seems resentful, rather than grateful, *after everything Capricorn Rising has done for them.* But "everything" may include pulling strings with Capricorn's contacts on behalf of the child.

After Mead "daydreamed" the future, "seeing" herself married (to Luther Cressman) and organizing church activities; married to "fellow anthropologist," (Reo Fortune, then planning to continue in psychology) and doing fieldwork with him; married to "sensitive" anthropologist (Gregory Bateson,) having a child and continuing with her work, all of it came to pass, temporarily.

But afterwards, her ex-husbands wondered, "how might my life have developed had I *not* met and married Margaret Mead?"

Mead's dissertation on Samoa became an overnight best seller. It brought her the unbelievable sum of $5,000 *during the Depression.* She had the funds for her next field trip with Reo. But two years later, when Reo's thesis was published as a trade book, he held it up and said sadly, "this is the last book that my name will be on *alone. Margaret's name* will be on everything else I publish for the rest of my life."

After the divorce, Mead wrote Reo's former professor in New Zealand, suggesting that Fortune needed a grant for a trip to China. Margaret didn't mention the divorce until A. R. Radcliffe-Brown replied, asking if she, too, needed funding for China. (He could help, but he needed to know the total amount.) He was surprised to learn that they were no longer married.[43]

After the divorce from Bateson, she also pulled strings on his behalf, angering his new wife. When told to stop manipulating, she expressed her concern about Cathy spending the summer with them. She thought Bateson impractical; she "wanted my daughter to have enough to eat."[44]

Mead's was an unusually dynamic horoscope with three Dignified planets on the Ascendant and Moon-in-Aquarius[45] (Detriment) in her Identity House. She was driven. It took the Museum of Natural History a decade to catalogue the 25,000 slides from the Bateson's field trip to Bali.

Back home, Mead enthusiastically planned an international conference for attendees from many different disciplines. She envisioned them all working together, studying a village that had a high percentage of schizophrenics. But World War II intervened and travel was restricted.

Gregory Bateson was exhausted; Bali was their last field trip together. After the divorce, Margaret said what she missed most was doing fieldwork with him.

---

43 Howard, cited above, pp 183-4.

44 In 1951 he married Betty Summer, a bishop's daughter and psychiatric nurse, in California.

45 The moon is in Detriment opposite *both* the Saturn-ruled Signs, Capricorn and Aquarius. In the Twelfth, First, or Second House, a Capricorn or Aquarius Moon will draw on the Creative Unconscious, (Twelfth,) Identity (First,) or means of earning a living and developing financial resources, (Second.)

The Element - Earth

Capricorn is the Zodiac's last Earth Sign. All the Earth Signs are practical, but Capricorn is the most pragmatic. Saturn's Rulership seems to accentuate the Element's patience. The other Earth Signs are hard-working too, but Capricorn endures in institutional settings. I once asked a Capricorn Rising administrator if she were the person who'd worked the longest in her department. "Yes, as a matter of fact," she said, "I am." She'd outlasted everyone else.

Capricorn's second home, the Institute, school, law firm, lab, corporation or committee is always in the back of their minds. In astrology sessions with them, I often think of Margaret Mead painstakingly collecting artifacts for her "museum home" on every field trip.

Capricorn is thorough. Mead's daughter, Catherine, remarked that hers was probably the best-documented childhood in the United States. Margaret had saved most of her childhood drawings!

Other Rising Signs also make contributions to knowledge, but this Ascendant seems to set higher personal standards. Influenced by her economist father, Edward Mead, who taught at the Wharton School of Finance and Commerce, Margaret believed the only worthwhile career was one in which she would "add to the world's sum of accurate information." She devoted herself to documenting cultures that were losing ground to trade, colonialism, missionary schools, and other modernizing influences.

But it wasn't simply about discovering "new,

accurate facts." The knowledge should also be useful to Mead's own culture. She asked questions like, "what can *American women* learn from the way babies are delivered in the Pacific islands? How does marriage work in other cultures? Is monogamy really the best way; should it be the only standard? Does Western culture lose something by giving up religious rituals which bring communities together?" Her *Redbook* columns, which discussed many of these topics, reached a wider readership than academic conferences.

As a teacher, Mead was also extremely practical. She didn't care that other professors laughed at her "role playing" classes for students who were about to leave for fieldwork. She wanted them to know how to use their new cameras; preserve their film in the tropics and charge their batteries. She knew an anthropologist who'd left his lens cap on, losing an entire ceremony in the islands. Her students also left with lists of local people who could help them, should they need help thousands of miles from home.

Similarly, Marie Curie believed classroom lectures should be practical. After Pierre died, Marie took over his classes at the University of Paris, and reporters attended her first session. They expected to hear Mrs. Curie's tribute to her late husband, but they were surprised. She launched right into the lecture on physics. Afterwards, she told them that Pierre had already been eulogized; the students were not there for that purpose. She herself had sat through many tedious lectures at the Sorbonne, filled with useless information and speculation. Students deserved better!

Social scientists like Mead and physicists like Curie are noted for their keen powers of observation, but Capricorn's strong Sensate Function comes through in the arts as well. James Joyce, who professed a belief in free love but had never had an affair, decided to set the scene for one in his novel, *Ulysses.*

He rented a hotel room, bought a certain type of clock for the mantel, and rearranged the furniture. He then invited a young woman, who thought she was going to an actual tryst with him, to the room. He observed every move she made as she walked around it. Then, he made an excuse and left. Later, he returned to rapidly write down the description of her dress, the scent of her perfume, her attitude; her general reaction to him and to the hotel. He did all this research for *one* scene!

Vita Sackville-West and Colleen McCullough both had a scientist's eye for observation and detail. Before they were writers, West was a noted horticulturist and McCullough did research in neurology. Colleen is perhaps best known for her novel, *Thorn Birds,* (sometimes called Australia's *Gone with the Wind,*) which exemplifies Capricorn's talent for creating atmosphere by a layering on of details. Readers feel as if they're present in the scene along with her characters.

When the Sensate Earth Element combines with lunar imagination and memory for detail, the result can be magical. McCullough has Jupiter-in-Fall in her First House, Pisces Moon in her Second, and Saturn conjunct the Nadir.

Ray Bradbury's short stories are atmospheric,

too. We can almost see the fireflies at twilight in summertime; taste the homemade dandelion wine in the ketchup bottles, smell the circus animals as they're unloaded from the train at five in the morning and hear the carnival eccentrics setting up their tents. We almost feel the cool mist over the ravines in Waukegan, Illinois.

Yeats gave a great deal of thought to his legacy, which poems would survive in his anthologies, and which would not. He was adamant that his various memoirs be called *Autobiographies,* in the plural. He polished every line of his poetry many times. The week before he died, Yeats was re-working *Under Ben Bulben* and *The Black Tower.*

The Earth Element is literal minded. Unless the Moon and Venus, the feminine planets, are strong by aspect and house position,[46] Capricorn can be quite judgmental. People who set high standards for themselves often wonder why others don't live up to those standards, too. They may, for example, resent paying taxes to help out fellow citizens who aren't as practical as they.

A high percentage of Air, for objectivity and humor, and Water planets for empathy and compassion, are helpful. Earth and Fire are a powerful combination, like a locomotive pulling a train down the track at top speed. Mead, Fonda and Bradbury had Sun-in-Fire; Yeats, Joyce and Mc Collough Sun-in-Air. Marie Curie had Sun-in-Water (Scorpio) and a Pisces Moon.

Capricorn Rising with five or more planets in

46 In the First House or near the Ascendant, the Feminine planets convey an impression of warmth and empathy.

Earth, including Mercury, or Capricorn Rising with difficult Saturn/Mercury or Saturn/Moon aspects, may indicate bouts of depression. Art Buchwald, Libra Sun with Saturn/Mercury conjunct, discussed his struggle with depression in print and on the Larry King show. Tipper Gore presented Buchwald with an award for his slogan, "don't commit suicide, because you might change your mind later."[47]

The Mode - Cardinality

Cardinal Masks contribute authority to the horoscope. Cardinality is a Yang, active Mode. The mode delegates work well, has organizing talent and helps in facilitating projects. Each of the four Cardinal Signs is associated with a different season; each is creative in a different way.[48] Capricorn is associated with professional and business creativity.

Because winter is "Capricorn's season," it's interesting that Margaret Mead chose *Blackberry Winter* for the title of her autobiography. "The colder the winter, the better the blackberries taste."

47 His mother was diagnosed with manic depression soon after his birth and hospitalized for thirty-five years. See, *Too Soon to Say Goodbye,* cited above, Chapter 7, "Depression." A sad consequence of Art's Earth/Air horoscope was that his friends misinterpreted his remarks about being suicidally depressed as "dark humor," not as a cry for help.

48 Capricorn and Cancer with the winter and summer Solstices; Aries and Libra with the spring and autumn Equinoxes. In the Western hemisphere, each Cardinal Sign coincides with a change in the weather.

The Capricorn Mask, through its association with the Tenth House (the pinnacle of success) and the steadfast Earth Element, is *particularly* authoritative. Capricorn's posture and gait (see "How to Recognize Capricorn," above) announce, "I'm in charge."

When Mead was a student at Barnard, teaching assistant Ruth Benedict informed her that others criticized the way she walked "with a spring in her step." A five-foot-tall woman preparing for a career in a man's field, Margaret wanted respect and intended to get it![49]

Leadership is a cardinal quality. As a child, Mead wrote plays to showcase her siblings' talents. Later, she took charge of her sisters' wardrobes before they left for college. She helped them to fit in at sororities. Margaret herself had designed her own college apparel, which drew laughter at De Pauw.[50] Rejected by two sororities, she spared her sisters that experience. Cardinal Rising leaders learn from their mistakes and make any needed adjustments. They seldom make the same mistake twice.

Yeats applied his organizing skills in the Irish nationalist movement and at the Abbey Theater,

---

49 *Blackberry Winter,* cited above, p.132. Her sisters married Leo Rosten, who wrote humorous stories about an immigrant's attempts to learn English, *(the Education of Hyman Kaplan),* and cartoonist William Steig.

50 Because her father had lost money on his investments, she didn't attend school on the East Coast. She went a year to his alma mater in the Midwest, De Pauw, where the students laughed at her East Coast pronunciation of "been" ("bean" instead of "bin.") Ser then transferred to Barnard, in the East.

which he and his patroness, Lady Augusta Gregory, founded. Comfortable in his leadership role at the Abbey, Yeats had a unique was of soothing theatrical egos. He'd walk on stage during rehearsal and slowly, dramatically intone the name of an Irish hero, for instance, "*Charles. Stewart. Parnell.*" Silenced, the cast and crew would stare at him, wondering, "what's this about Parnell?" Once Yeats had their attention, he proceeded to resolve the dispute, which had nothing at all to do with the beloved hero.

The most competitive Mode, Cardinality hates to fail. *Capricorn* Cardinality, though, is sometimes inspired by failure. Tennessee Williams would rush to his typewriter, energized by a bad review. When critics said his play "didn't work," he accepted their verdict, immediately responded to the challenge and fixed it. "A bad review can be more useful than a good one," he once remarked.

In the Master's program at the University of Chicago, one of my classmates received a B+ on a seminar paper. Furious because she'd never received anything less than an A as an undergraduate, she confronted the professor after class. She demanded to know what, besides "that unhelpful criticism at the top of the paper," she'd need to do to change her grade. The rest of us looked on in admiration as the professor became flustered, then made several suggestions.

An astrology student at the time, I calculated her chart and discovered she had Capricorn Rising with several Cardinal planets opposed and in square to the Ascendant. *She intended to succeed,* and she did. The next time our class met, she dropped her paper, including several rewritten pages, on the professor's desk.

Astrology teachers are sometimes asked if Cardinal Earth is ruthless, given its Saturnian discipline, focus, pragmatism and competitive nature. The answer is, *the entire horoscope must be considered.* In a chart with Saturn-in-Rulership *or* Mars Exalted, —and Margaret Mead had both— the Identity House (First) *does* seeks to control life, and the person may well be called "domineering" by his or her competition and former spouse.

However, if there's a First House Moon and/or a Mutable Sun Sign—Mead and Yeats had both—or, if Jupiter is strong—Mead's was conjunct her Ascendant—then empathy and generosity will counterbalance the problem-solving Mars or the ambitious Saturn. They're more generous; *they expand their ambitions to include others' success.*[51]

The more planets there are in the First House, the more complex the personality. Moon-in-Cancer or Pisces (like Marie Curie's) indicates sympathy and/or empathy.

The more aspects there are to the Ascendant degree, the more complex the personality. Though English astrologer, poet laureate, essayist, playwright and courtier John Dryden had no planets *in* his First House, five planets *aspected* Dryden's Ascendant degree. His was a complicated life. Successful under Oliver Cromwell, the Great Protector, Dryden changed

51 "Who shall I have on my committee? Who shall I include in the grant proposal? It's interesting that Mead saw competitiveness as "based on envy."

religions when a Catholic dynasty came to power in 1680, (the "Glorious Revolution") then lost influence when it fell. The inventor of the "heroic couplet," Dryden may have left us the most practical essay in the English language about writing.[52]

Even without First House planets, the Capricorn Mask is authoritative. In fact, if there are no First House planets (or no Earth planets) in the horoscope, this Mask may overcompensate by trying even harder to achieve.

Cardinal Masks are more adaptable than Fixed but less flexible than Mutable. World War II and its aftermath affected several of the Capricorn Rising examples; it's interesting to observe how they coped.

Mead's plans for an interdisciplinary, international study of remote Pacific villages were interrupted and finally cancelled; social scientists lost interest in working with people outside their area of expertise. Her husband Gregory's life took off in a different direction during the War; they divorced afterwards. Divorce was more difficult for Mead this time, because *he* was the one who left. However, with Sun in Mutability (Sagittarius,) she quickly adjusted, immersing herself in seminars, museum administration and government service. She wrote a beautiful poem[53] expressing her feelings about letting go.

World War II brought Art Buchwald to Paris, where he left his "Marine family" and began his career as a journalist. With Mutable (Sagittarius) Moon/Venus, he, too, adapted well to change.

52 It's in the introduction to his book, *Fables.*

53 Untitled, it's at the end of *Blackberry Winter.*

Ireland became independent at the end of the War. In the new democracy, life changed for Yeats and his friends, the Anglo-Irish elite. Outnumbered by Roman Catholics, they lost power. Though Yeats had worked for Home Rule as a young man, some of the post-war changes saddened him. The poet wrote, "Ireland is a nation now, but I have lost my country."

After a series of sorrowful poems, he, too, adapted. Yeats became the "smiling public man of sixty," as he described himself in "Among School Children," while serving in the Senate. He had a Mutable (Gemini) Sun Sign.

The Mask in Youth
Lunar Imagination Helps Transcend Saturn's Sense of Limitation

In youth, Jane Fonda's conventional Mask stifled her Sagittarian Sun.

> I was brought up in such a restricted kind of way, you know, one doesn't raise one's voice, one never shows what one feels, one is always polite. If someone said something to me that I didn't like, I would never show it.

Like Fonda, many of my clients with the Sagittarius/ Capricorn Rising combination had parents who used the rules of etiquette to distance themselves from their own feelings and their childrens' feelings, too. In her career as a method actress, where drawing on one's emotions is a major part of the process, Jane found her family's approach a liability.

At the age of thirty-three, after the Saturn Return, while researching her role in the movie, *Tall Story*, Jane discovered Freudian analysis. When she mentioned it to her father, Henry Fonda told her she "needed analysis like a hole in the head."[54] Yet, she learned from therapy that "an actor's performance is blocked by the same issues that block the actor as a human being." After analysis, her Leo Sun was able to speak out, regardless of social conventions. In her three marriages, however, Jane still found it difficult to tell her husbands what she needed from them. She was afraid of losing their love.

And, too, her Leo nature became caught up in the action, first in Tom Hayden's political career, then later, in giving parties and traveling from ranch to ranch and back to Atlanta with Ted Turner. Owning twenty houses left her "feeling rootless!" She missed her children, whom she saw only when they managed to connect along the Turners' travel route. While in Nebraska and New Mexico, she also missed her "energizing" volunteer work in Georgia.

Margaret Mead developed both her feminine side *and* her very ambitious masculine side. Her relationship with her father brought her a useful skill, *the ability to negotiate.* She used it throughout her career.

Whenever her father promised to attend a school

54 He thought her too self-absorbed as it was and didn't see her insecurity.

performance, but *didn't*, her brother Dick and her grandmother were more upset than she. She knew that at the last minute he'd "beg off," but he always gave her a dollar the next day. She could *depend* on that dollar! "Only love," she said, "is irreplaceable; *everything else is negotiable.*[55]

Later, as a successful professional, whenever Mead wanted a grant for herself, a student or an ex-husband, she'd call an organization and negotiate. She'd promise to come and speak at their conference or to give lectures at their university if they, in turn, would help her candidate with his grant.

Her First Saturn Return was very difficult. She later wrote that she'd never in her life been as lonely or unhappy as she was on her thirtieth birthday, spent in a primitive village suffering from a broken ankle. Her husband, Reo Fortune, had gone away with the village men for several months. Shortly afterwards, she met Gregory Bateson.

In Ray Bradbury's childhood, every Fourth of July his grandfather was the "priest of the magical fireworks' ritual" and Ray was "his altar boy." Like Fonda, Bradbury had a Fire Sun Sign. Theater was also Ray's creative outlet in youth, though he began in radio. When his family lived for a short time, in Tucson, Arizona, Ray told the other boys that he'd soon be hired at the radio station. "What? That's stupid! *You're only twelve!*" they said. Ray then volunteered to run errands at the station, was accepted, and before long was doing voices on the "Katzenjammer Kids" radio program.

55 *Blackberry Winter*, 77.

At thirteen, when his father found a job in Los Angeles, Ray roller-skated to Paramount Studio, met George Burns and wrote several jokes for the comedian. Next, he turned up at the Wiltshire Theater, in his thick glasses, long hair and shabby apparel, demanding a role. The woman in charge, who had her choice of attractive, fashionably dressed young people, including trained actors, said she had nothing for him. "Oh, but you *have to* hire me! I've already told my friends I'm working here," he said. And she did.

Though he always loved the theater—he'd own one later in life— Bradbury soon discovered his real talents lay in writing fantasy and science fiction.

Like many with Capricorn Rising, in his thirties, Ray took on a difficult project, the *Moby Dick* screenplay, with a difficult director, John Huston, known in Hollywood for ridiculing underlings and expecting the impossible. Like Bradbury, my Capricorn Rising clients often choose the most challenging degree programs, the most demanding professors, and the most difficult universities.

Ray decided to take on the enormous project[56] because "if you work with John Huston *and you succeed,* you'll never be without work again in Hollywood." He was right. After *Moby Dick,* Bradbury's reputation was established. By thirty-six, he'd won job security in a town of highly talented, very competitive people. Young Ray was a long term planner.

Yeats remarked on how difficult it was to fully immerse himself in the rituals and symbolism of the

56 He later based his story, *Green Shadows and White Whales,* on the experience.

Golden Dawn Society (which influenced his early poetry, *Celtic Twilight* and *Wandering Aengus,*[57]) because his father's skeptical voice lingered in the back of his mind. His father's views also interfered with his attempts at what is now called Active Imagination.

While dialoguing on paper with the spirit guide, "Leo Africanus,"[58] he became distracted by concern as to whether or not his spirit guide was an actual historical figure. Yeats stopped his imaginative process to research Leo's life "as a poet from Fez," then gave up on him.

Many Capricorns who, like Yeats, have studied astrological symbolism, mythology and spiritual techniques, remark that these pursuits enhanced their imagination, intuition and creativity. For Yeats, they were also an important part of the journey to Wholeness.

When Yeats was thirty-seven, Maud, his muse, converted to Catholicism and married the war hero, John Mac Bride. As a Catholic, she'd never be free to divorce. Yeats was devastated.[59] He wrote a poem to send her away—stating that she could only "burn down his Troy" *once*—and began to see other women,

57 Solar and lunar imagery. Ellmann, cited above, 106; Yeats *Journal*, with astrology notes.

58 Yeats wrote his questions on one side of his notebook and Leo's "answers" on the opposite page.

59 Ellmann 182-3. In 1907 he wrote, "I fear that I have lost—my center as it were—has shifted from its natural interests, and that it will take me a long time finding myself again." And the lines, (Maud had taken,) "All till my youth was gone/ Without a pitying look,/How shall I praise that one?" 166.

actress Florence Farr and Olivia Shakespear, ("Diane Vernon.")

His "spiritual marriage" to Maud Gonne and his long marriage to Georgia Hyde-Lees were important to Yeats' creative development. He seemed closest to women who shared his esotericl interests, Maud, Florence Farr, and his wife, Georgia.[60]

At forty-three, Yeats met Ezra Pound, his brash, young American secretary who introduced him to Noh plays, convinced him to "modernize" his style, come out of the *Celtic Twilight* "into the Twentieth Century;" write tersely, drop those abstractions and go for the emotions!

James Joyce's long relationship with Nora Barnacle, the prototype for Molly Bloom, grounded him and also stimulated his imagination. An alcoholic who wandered across Europe with his wife and two children, Joyce saw Nora as his "Ireland" and his anchor.

Margaret Mead was forty-seven when Gregory Bateson left her. But Ruth Benedict's death the same year seemed to affect her more.

It's interesting that Fonda, Buchwald, and Mead all had Jupiter-in-Fall on, or close to, the Ascendant. While it's true that their hard work resulted in success, *they also had their share of Jupiter's good luck.* Buchwald ended World War II in Paris as a stringer for the *Herald Tribune.* Fonda won roles worthy of Oscars. Mead always found ritual events in 'her' villages to write about, while others fieldworkers might be six months

60 She agreed to call herself "George" before the wedding because he and Ezra Pound decided it was easier to rhyme than Georgia.

in a village not far from Margaret's and find nothing worth documenting.

The Mask After Midlife Beyond Insecurity and Vain Regrets - Forgiving Others, Forgiving Self

John Greenleaf Whittier, a Capricorn Rising poet, wrote, "For all sad words of tongue and pen/the saddest are/ It might have been."

At fifty, in "Man and His Echo," Yeats described something many of us have experienced. He woke in the middle of the night with regretful thoughts and had difficulty getting back to sleep.

The poet wrote:

All that I have said and done

Now that I am old and ill,

Turns into a question till

I lie awake night after night

And never get the answers right.

Did those words of mine send out

Certain men the English shot?

Though we haven't written plays encouraging young men to risk their lives for Irish independence, by fifty most of us have had similar experiences. We've had our share of vain regrets. The road to hell is also said to be paved with *those,* along with good intentions! In the middle of the night, we, too, may come to terms with the human condition. And, like Yeats, we don't always "get the answers right."[61]

During a TV interview with Barbara Walters when she was fifty-one, Jane Fonda apologized to Vietnam veterans and their families for her "careless and thoughtless remarks" made during the anti-war protests of 1972. She came to realize that her anger over the war and her empathy for the suffering people in Hanoi didn't excuse her hurtful words.

On a personal level, the Chiron Return (around the age of fifty) connects sensitive people with their inner "wounded healer." This seems particularly true in the healing professions. Many Capricorn Rising people, in attending to others' needs, have put their own needs on hold.

When Tom Hayden ended their sixteen-year marriage, Jane Fonda felt wounded and vulnerable. She missed the "usness" and the holiday traditions.[62] She surrounded herself with women friends, went into therapy and read *Leaving My Father's House,* by Jungian analyst Marion Woodman.

Slowly, Jane "grew a membrane over the wound."

---

61 In his astrology journal, Part II of *Memoirs,* (London, Macmillan,) 1977. Yeats also regretted not taking the stage in defense of his friend, playwright J.M. Synge as his father did, "ignoring the craven men hiding in the gallery, Diary entry 50, about progressions to his Natal Mars.

62 She'd really enjoyed dressing up as the Easter Bunny every year with the family around her.

She learned that Woodman was right; vulnerability *did* open to humility. Three years later she married Ted Turner. (Fire Sun Signs move on faster than the other Elements.) Fonda resolved to work on her fear of intimacy. Unfortunately, she chose a man with the same problem.[63]

Sometimes, in their fifties, Capricorn Rising suffers from an illness like Yeats, ("now that I am old and ill') and become more aware of their waning vitality. But productive, purposeful Capricorn still sees so much to be done. What is this fatigue, this lack of vitality? When will my energy return? In "Lines Written in Dejection," Yeats expressed it well,

> The holy centaurs of the hills are vanished;
>
> I have nothing but the embittered sun;
>
> Banished heroic mother moon and vanished,
>
> And now that I have come to fifty years
>
> I must endure the timid sun.

And he continued working in spite of the "dejection," throwing himself into the play, "At the Hawk's Well."[64]

---

63 Fonda had lost her mother to suicide; Ted's father was also a suicide. She and Turner both feared abandonment.

64 For Yeats, (Sun-in-Gemini,) the hawk was a symbol of "the mind's eye" and the analytical thinking process. In his astrology journal (*Memoirs* Part II,) he lamented constantly stopping to analyze instead of following his instincts and impulses. He "should have" defended Lady Gregory's son Robert; he wished he'd been more spontaneous on many occasions. Ellmann, pp.215-16.

Astrologers will appreciate the symbolism. Chiron is, of course, a "heroic," youthful, energetic centaur. But Yeats and his friends were getting older. "Heroic Mother Moon" is banished. Maud Gonne, who'd rallied large crowds in her youth, was forbidden by the British government to return to Ireland. And when she came back in disguise, she looked older. A Sagittarius Sun Sign, Maud was represented by both the Centaur and "The Arrow," the title of Yeats' poem which ends, "This beauty's kinder, yet for a reason/ I could weep/ That *the old is out of season*"

The timid sun in "Lines Written in Dejection" is the Ego, the Sun Sign. At fifty, our "half century birthday," many of us exhale deeply, as if subconsciously releasing the Ego's unfinished desires and, often, its responsibility for grown children.

A few Capricorn Rising clients, nearly all of them women, have embarked on an advanced degree at fifty or have adopted a grandchild. A few male clients have decided, like Yeats, that they want heirs, married younger women and started new families in their fifties. But that's unusual. Most are ready to leave parenting and career responsibilities behind.

At the end of his fiftieth year, Yeats had a mystical experience. His wife said it "remained with him all his life." He wrote this verse about it:

> My fiftieth year had come and gone,
>
> I sat, a solitary man,
>
> In a crowded London shop,
>
> An open book and empty cup

On the marble table-top.
While on the shop and street I gazed
My body of a sudden blazed;
And twenty minutes more or less
It seemed, so great my happiness,
That I was blessed and could bless.[65]

At fifty-two, the poet married for the first and only time. During his honeymoon with Georgia Hyde-Lees, (then studying Rudolph Steiner's esoteric teachings,) he was finally able to suspend his skepticism about the supernatural.

One night, his bride tried automatic writing.[66] Decades later, she told Yeats' biographer, Richard Ellmann, that her new husband was sad and moody over his rejection by Iseult Gonne.[67] To distract him, Georgia picked up a pencil and wrote a few cryptic phrases. Then, suddenly, the pencil began to move on its own, producing ideas, symbols, and sketches. Yeats was excited! He remained enthusiastic about the

65 The long poem was originally called "Wisdom," but Yeats changed the title to "Vacillations," the verse is from Part IV. In his astrology Journal (*Memoirs*, Part II) he attributes his skepticism to his "Moon in Saturn's Sign," (Aquarius,) as well as to his father's influence.

66 Ellmann, cited above, xvi-xvii. The first version (1926) was very close to the automatic writing. He realized he needed more time to digest the information. The posthumous second version has the preface.

67 Maud Gonne's daughter. See below.

automatic writing and the spirits who guided Georgia for years. He never needed to attend another séance.

An "oath bound man,"[68] Yeats was compelled to silence about occult techniques. But shortly before his death, he credited Georgia and her spirit collaborators with much of the material in a new preface to *A Vision.*

He wrote to the printer that he'd wrestled with the symbolism "like Homer's Odysseus had wrestled with Proteus, the Old Man of the Sea," and that he, too, needed to "get home to Ithica." By his seventies, *A Vision's* revolving gyres, the opposites, had come to symbolize Man and God; Life and Death. The unity or integration in the Thirteenth Phase of the Moon, indicated that the poet had "come home" to himself. He said that if he were young again, he'd write more about *Unity.*

Happy to leave administrative work at the Abbey Theater to the younger generation, Yeats also resigned from the Senate in his early sixties "because of ill health." Content with his work, his wife and two young children, the poet was surprised to learn that according to the critics, he was "doing his best work" in his old age! Like Yeats, many people with Capricorn Rising are happiest in the prime of life, after the Second Saturn Return.

In her fifties, Mead wrote that she'd "reached the age of committees;" she served on governmental,

---

68 Yeats' used the phrase several times in "The Black Tower," written at the end of his life. He also used the past tense, as if he was no longer "oath bound," possibly because he'd left the Golden Dawn.

academic, and international councils. She taught seminars preparing anthropologists for field work. She'd written thirty-nine books and contributed to another eighteen. Too old for field work, she'd become a household word at home. She enjoyed mentoring graduate students.

Her practical articles and advice columns in *Redbook* magazine were widely read. During her travels, she stopped to see her daughter's family in Iran. Mead's visit to the Pacific was celebrated by village elders, who remembered her from long ago and had composed a song in her honor.

Like Yeats, Capricorn Rising may experience the "timid sun" at fifty. However, like Margaret Mead, after the menopause, many women, feel renewed "zest and enthusiasm" at sixty. This will depend, of course, on whether Natal Jupiter is in an angular house (1, 4, 7, 10) or makes aspects to Natal planets. If so, the Natal House and aspects are energized at sixty.

Mead and Fonda both experienced the Jupiter Return on their Ascendant; and they both seem to have felt the zest. Excited about new ideas, Mead took out her notebook at dinner parties and jotted them down for lectures and articles. Fonda focused on her Foundation and on spirituality.

Jupiter symbolizes contentment and generosity of spirit. Fonda forgave her mother for abandoning her and, afterwards, had an easier time forgiving herself.

A chapter of her memoir, *My Life So Far* is called, "Sixty."[69]

During the Second Saturn Return, she watched her forty-nine films and old home movies from her childhood. Observing "the continuity" of her life helped Jane "prepare for Act III," which began at sixty.

The Jupiter Return often coincides with renewed interest in spirituality and/or a desire to expand in new directions. Fonda felt "led," or guided by a Higher Power, during her divorces with Hayden and Turner. An openness to grace is an asset in healing old wounds.

Sometimes, however, Capricorn's spouse is ill-equipped for change or disinterested in it. When Jane asked for "a voice" in her marriage, her request frightened Ted Turner. An atheist, he was already disturbed by her new interest in Christianity.[70]

Art Buchwald also had Jupiter in the First House. At sixty, he too experienced the Jupiter Return in his Identity House. However, he was hospitalized for severe depression at sixty-three. And in his eighties,

---

69 She also regretted not having been a better mother and not having found the time for spiritual interests. She wrote that "out of regret comes restitution;" her foundation focuses on preventing pregnancy and improving the quality of life of adolescent girls.

70 He began looking for her replacement. When she was sixty-two, the couple divorced.

he still found it difficult to forgive others for his childhood suffering.[71]

Though all the examples faced challenges during the First Half of Life, Fonda and Mead began a new, relaxed, expansive and fulfilling cycle at sixty.[72] Bradbury was in great demand, writing for radio, TV, the movies and as the Future Pavilion designer for the World's Fair. Yeats "did his best work" and was happy in his marriage. While Buchwald remained as prolific and productive as ever, he wasn't as contented as the others at sixty.

The Aquarian Progressed Mask - Uniqueness and Risk

Aquarius is Fixed Air and usually presents a more sociable *persona* than Natal Capricorn. Detachment, objectivity, originality (unique talents) and openness to risk are developed during this thirty-year-cycle.

By midlife, Capricorn Rising clients often tell me their workday feels like Hercules' task of mucking out the Augean stables. Divorce attorneys, doctors, nurses,

71 The humorist concluded his book *Too Soon to Say Goodbye*, "but if nothing else, I know I made an awful lot of people happy, " (cited above, 146.) Like so many other peoples,' this memoir, written at the end of his life, discussed his regrets.

72 On her "Jupiter Return year" birthday, Fonda's third husband, Ted Turner surprised her with "the gift that keeps on giving," for her 60th birthday, a $10,000,000 family foundation. Through the grant, she and each of her children have been able to promote the cause of their choice.

social workers, teachers and administrators have all said they're tired of cleaning up others' messes.

By Midlife, Capricorn Rising professionals are tired of "romantics who, after four divorces, still refuse pre-nuptial agreements;" or "morbidly obese patients who, year-after-year, refuse to change their diet," or "clients who prefer pills to doing their inner work," or "parents who won't turn off video games and supervise children's homework."

Productive and prolific like the examples in this chapter, they'd like to free themselves from their routines. However, they're also concerned about their pensions! If, during the Aquarius mask-building phase, Capricorn became comfortable with risk and excited about learning new things, and if those risks worked out well for Capricorn, he's more likely to welcome an adventure after fifty.

As soon as they progress into Aquarius,[73] Capricorns begin to transcend their "Saturn" fears, embarrassment and other insecurities. They begin developing the confidence needed for their adult contributions to society (House Eleven.)

This was an interesting progression for Yeats and Mead, as both had the Natal Sun/Uranus conjunction. They resonated to the ruler of the new cycle, Uranus. Both also had Aquarian planets intercepted in the First House; they "found themselves" (assimilated

---

73 The age of ingress depends upon the *degree* on the Natal Ascendant, Yeats was one year old; Bradbury eight, Fonda fifteen and Curie eighteen.

these planets) through the creative imagination, in childhood, they wrote poetry and plays.[74]

The Aquarius Mask leaves its imprint on Capricorn's youth and young adulthood. An Air Sign, Aquarius favors writing and learning. The Mask may bring out the creative flair of a First or Second House planet in Aquarius.[75] If the progressed Mask aspects Natal Uranus (ruler of Aquarius) while moving through the First House, Capricorn Rising may discover a unique talent.

A Fixed Sign, Aquarius accentuates will power. Because Yeats was born with *the last degree* of Capricorn Rising, Aquarius became his new progressed Mask when he was a year old. A few years later, little Willie's father found him "stubborn and resistant" about learning to read; the boy preferred listening to ghost stories in the kitchen with the help!

Aquarius represents the Eleventh House Archetype of friendship and group interactions. It's the archetype of *belonging.* Several Capricorn Rising women have told me *long after midlife* about college experiences similar to Margaret Mead's, experiences that still rankled. They'd all wanted very much to belong to a

---

74 Mead wrote a play at De Pauw which the school performed. The sororities "noticed her" afterwards but she'd lost interest in them. Yeats and a school friend wrote a play together in Ireland.

75 Though Bradbury had no Natal planets in Aquarius, he began writing stories on butcher paper at eleven. His teachers encouraged him. At thirteen, the progressed Aquarian Ascendant aspected two Virgo planets, (Venus and Saturn) by inconjunct.

sorority, so they "bid" several "Greek" organizations, only to be rejected by them all.

However, in the process, they discovered that they didn't fit the conventional mold! There was something "different' about them that sorority leaders feared or disliked. They were "too intellectual," "too foreign-looking," or, like Mead, didn't purchase their clothing at the right stores.[76]

First House planets are connected to one's sense of Self. Several women clients with strong Uranus aspects but different Rising Signs, for instance, have had similar experiences to Mead's. But when asked about sororities, they'll usually laugh about being rejected. It wasn't a particularly painful memory. One woman said, "I learned I was a *trend-setter,* not a follower!"

Like Mead, she, too, had transferred to a university where she "fit in" and was happy. But for Capricorn Rising, an Ascendant that values tradition, rules, and conventionality, to be seen as "different" comes as a shock! But it also clarifies *who they are,* in contrast to those who reject them!

It's helpful to look at the house where Natal Uranus, the planet ruling this developmental phase, is located. That House symbolizes the way in which their "uniqueness" will later become an asset. Mead's Sun/Uranus conjunction was in her Eleventh House. (Aquarius in the Natural Zodiac.) Her *potential,* her international (Sun/Uranus in Sagittarius) role as a

76 Mead, with Venus-in-Aquarius in the First, had designed her own dresses. The other girls all dressed in the latest trend, and bought their clothing in the same stores. Margaret helped her younger sisters avoid her mistake.

cultural interpreter was not seen in the Midwest. Nor would it have been appreciated by girls who wanted to associate with those who looked and thought as they did; who spoke with a similar Midwestern accent.

Bradbury's Aquarian mask formed a trine with his Sun-in-Leo; Fonda's and Mead's sextiled their Sagittarian Suns. Buchwald's Aquarian mask sextiled his Tenth House Libra Sun. This cycle brings out the more Yang Air and Fire Natal planets.

Young Marie Sklowdowska,[77] however, had a square between the progressed Mask and her Natal Scorpio Sun. When she progressed into Aquarius, she was working as a governess in Poland. She fell in love with the son and heir of the noble house, but her story had a sad ending. He was unable to tell his parents he wanted to marry a servant. Maria told him that she was glad she "hadn't married a coward!" She moved to Paris and immersed herself in science. With Uranus on her Seventh House cusp, she said later in life, that "in a sense I was married to Science."

When, on Mead's thirtieth birthday, she felt the "worse depression I've ever experienced," her progressed Ascendant was in twenty-eight degrees Capricorn. For her, the end of the long progressed cycle coincided with the Saturn Return. She was in a remote village; her husband having "gone off with the men."

This combination of a Saturn Return with the progressed Ascendant changing Signs sometimes feels like the darkest hours of the night, the hours that preceed the dawn of a new cycle.

77 Curie's maiden name.

The Pisces Progressed Mask - Imagination, Intuition, Vision

By the end of the Aquarian cycle, most Capricorns have assimilated some Airy objectivity. Curie's move to Paris after her failed romance is one example. Mead, with Venus and Moon-in-Aquarius, detached and moved on in her personal and professional life. My California clients tend to follow this pattern, many have moved cross-country, or, like Curie, from abroad.

Pisces is Mutable Water. William Butler Yeats was a late bloomer, like many Gemini Sun Sign people. He entered the thirty-year Pisces cycle much more objective about his writing than his personal life. The Yeats family lived in London and sometimes spent summers in Ireland. Though artists and other talented people came to visit his father, young Willie wrote his Irish friends about his "terrible loneliness" in England.

Then, one day when he was twenty-four, (a Jupiter Return year) the "stunningly beautiful" Maud Gonne paid the family a visit.[78] With the aid of his Piscean poet- *persona,* Yeats, the young man who ordinarily hesitated, analyzed, and was of two minds about nearly everything, took a risk and invited her to dinner the next evening. Miss Gonne accepted; they immediately

---

78 January 20, 1889. Yeats' sister Elizabeth described Maud in her diary as "keeping the hansom cab waiting during the visit" and "wearing slippers instead of shoes." She said that all the young men in Dublin were smitten with Maud. And *Willle* had asked her to dinner!

became friends. She was to remain his muse and his obsession for fifteen years [79]

When they met, Yeats' progressed Ascendant was conjunct his First House Chiron (the Wounded Healer.) Over the next ten years, the Pisces Ascendant slowly formed a Mutable T-square to the Natal Sun/ Uranus conjunction in his Fifth House (romance) and Jupiter (in Rulership) in his Eleventh. Finally, the Pisces Mask formed an inconjunct to his North Node/ Saturn conjunction in the Eighth (others peoples' secrets, values, needs and resources.)

As the Ascendant brought out *his own Natal planets*, Yeats saw Maud as exciting and stimulating, (Uranus) kind and spiritual, (Jupiter,) as someone who "understood him (Sun/ego) better than anyone else." And yet, she was *unattainable.* She lived in Paris, where he sometimes visited her; she was in and out of his life (Uranus) in London and Ireland.

He later wondered, was she loving or was she cold? (Saturn.) Did he see the real woman or the beautiful Mask, the *persona* of the inspiring speaker at nationalist ralleys. In his poem, "The Mask;" the lover poses the questions and the Mask responds.

While the previous Uranus-ruled cycle, brought clarity to Capricorn, the Neptune-ruled Pisces cycle is more likely to be confusing. For Yeats, the symbols and rites of the Golden Dawn, spirit guides met in séances (Leo Africanus and others) and poetry were useful

79 Though he twice asked her to marry him, unfortunately for Yeats, Maud, the daughter of a former military officer, (by then a diplomatic attaché,) preferred men of action to poets and mystics.

ways of delving into the Unconscious and sorting things out. In Yeats' mind, his muse was a virgin sacrificing herself for her cause, Irish independence. On some level he must have suspected Maud of having a secret life in Paris, though she didn't tell him about it for many years. (By then, he'd progressed into Aries Rising.)

Whether Capricorn Rising's work involves the arts, sciences, professions, administration or property development (Saturn is fortunate with land and property) the Pisces cycle expands and enhances their vision. Jupiter, the largest planet in the Solar System, ruled Pisces for centuries, before Neptune was discovered and has its effect. It symbolizes big dreams.

Marie Curie's Natal Pisces Moon in her Second House was probably conjunct her husband Pierre's Ascendant, though his birth data seems not to be as accurate as hers. Years older than she, Pierre saw the potential of her student research. As physicists, they shared the same vision— that gamma rays would benefit humanity— and dedicated their lives to it. They were right, radium had definite practical uses.

Curie is the least materialistic of the Capricorn Rising examples.[80] She and Pierre(Pisces Rising) refused to patent their discoveries, stating that "the knowledge belongs to science, not to us." Pierre

80 See the list of quotes at the beginning of Capricorn Rising. Albert Einstein said that fame hadn't changed her at all. Her Pisces Moon had an impact.

died three years after they won the Nobel Prize[81] in physics, leaving Marie a widow with two children at thirty-nine. Though women were not admitted to the Academy of Sciences, she was given Pierre's classes at the University of Paris.

Like Mead in anthropology and Curie in physics and chemistry, the imaginative Pisces cycle also results in success in the arts and entertainment. Pisces forms a symbolic sextile (opportunity aspect) to Capricorn Rising. Neptune, ruler of Pisces, is a visionary ruling planet.

Three years into the Pisces progression, Ray Bradbury's Ascendant conjuncted Uranus, his only First House planet. (It was almost in his Second.) His science fiction book, *The Martian Chronicles* appeared that year. Ray became famous in the genre at thirty.

"Dandelion Wine" followed, with its subtle message about prohibition. *Fahrenheit 452,* on censorship, appeared next. Two decades later, in the 1970's, Bradbury wrote the screenplay for *Moby Dick,* which became a successful movie. Christopher Isherwood's reviews of his stories helped establish Bradbury's reputation as a Hollywood screenwriter.

Jane Fonda graduated from movies like Barbarella to more challenging roles. She received an Oscar for *Klute.*

---

81 They won it for their radium discovery in 1903, sharing the prize with Lucien Berquerel, who also studied gamma rays.

The Aries Progression - New Beginnings

Aries is Cardinal Fire, Mars-ruled, and squares Natal Capricorn. Capricorn Rising enters the Aries' progression after Midlife, when careers are well established. Ray Bradbury, for instance, had written for radio and the movies earlier. Then, during the Aries progression, he began adapting his stories for television. He wrote for "The Bradbury Show" and revised "I Sing the Body Electric" for "The Twilight Zone."

Similarly, many clients and friends have reinvented themselves; reworked old articles and other material, learned to blog and published online newsletters about their current interests and causes. The internet is fast becoming their new medium the way television became Bradbury's.

Mars symbolizes energy. Margaret Mead experienced renewed vitality (zest) at sixty during the Mars-ruled (Aries) progression. Often progressions coincide with and enhance planetary cycles like the Jupiter Return.

Mars is also the planet of discovery. Marie Curie received a second Nobel Prize in 1911, this time in chemistry, for isolating the new element, Polonium.[82] She soon put the prize money to use, purchasing war bonds and financing x-ray machines. A hundred mobile ambulances were fitted with the technology and dispatched from Paris to the front.

82 Curie disproves the rule that scientists and mathematicians lose their creativity by thirty.

Curie talked doctors into taking x-rays and taught them how to use the machines. At first, they resisted; they saw no need to "waste time" with new technology while wounded soldiers awaited surgery. But Marie patiently demonstrated the equipment and proved that x-rays could quickly locate the exact place for an incision. And smaller, more precise cuts reduced the risk of infection. The doctors were finally convinced.

Marie even drove an ambulance herself. One day, it went into a ditch. She climbed out, covered with bruises. The next morning, Marie sent for an ambulance in better repair and set forth again! For Curie, wartime sacrifice was not financial or physical, but "my lost hours in the lab."

These Capricorn Rising examples were (and are) characterized by their vision and strong convictions. Each responded to "their" war (the Mars/Aries theme) in their own way, and each influenced the culture through their work.

Bradbury, who'd decided in youth not to fight but to "live for his country," helped develop a new mythology for the Space Age. Fonda, like her second husband Tom Hayden, held strong anti-war convictions, though she later apologized for the words she chose to express them.

Yeats became known as Ireland's national poet, "the poet of the Revolution." Future generations of school children would recite his poems with pride, particularly, "Easter 1916" which ended, "a terrible beauty is born."[83]

He mentioned his strong (Seventh House) Mars several times in *Memoirs.* Yeats was well aware of the extremes to which the "god of war" can go.[84] His poem, "Remorse for Intemperate Speech" (1931) ends with, "Out of Ireland have we come/Great hatred, little room/Maimed us at the start/ I carried from my mother's womb/A fanatic's heart."

Mead also had an angular Mars, but hers was Exalted and conjunct the Ascendant degree. She seems to have fought her generation's war (World War II) as a Pacific regional analyst for the US Government, though the information is still classified. While living in Washington D.C, she and other social scientists involved in the war effort organized a commune in rural New York for their children,[85] whom they visited whenever possible. Applying her fieldwork knowledge at home, Mead demonstrated that a village can, when necessary, raise a child.

For Capricorn Rising, both inner and outer battles seem to characterize the Mars-ruled Aries progression. Fonda won a second Oscar, this time for *Coming*

83 His friend and critic, Maud Gonne, liked the ending, but not the beginning. The stone, in her view, was not a good image for a patriotic poem.

84 He believed his Mars was seen as "irritable and arrogant" and resulted in trouble with others.

85 Sometimes one parent worked in Washington while the other lived in New York with their children. However, neither of Catherine Bateson's parents could live with the group full time. Margaret visited as many weekends as she could.

Home, a movie about the Vietnam War. But she still struggled with insecurity and fear of abandonment; she had to "work up the courage" to tell her husbands what she wanted and needed *for herself.* She also appeared with her father in *On Golden Pond*, a film on love and loyalty, about "a withholding father and his angry daughter."[86]

At thirty-seven, Yeats learned of Maud's secret life. He'd barely recovered from the fact that his "virginal ideal," whom he'd believed celibate and sublimating her energy into Irish nationalism, had in fact been the longtime mistress of French politician Lucien Millevoye. She shared this with Yeats "as she sat sobbing by the fire." After having two children with her lover, (Iseult and a son who died,) Maud was dumped in favor of a new mistress. Yeats was first stunned, then sad for her, and, finally, outraged.

However, the worst blow came a few years later, when he received the telegram announcing her marriage to John Mac Bride, who Yeats considered "a lout" and "a clown." The poet went from shock to fury, lashing out at Maud in his journal and poems. He wrote to others that she had led him on, that she "consumed my youth." Surprised at this reaction, Maud told others she'd "done nothing of the kind!"

---

86 Jane quoted a line in the film, "we all do the best we can." Jane got Henry Fonda his part in the movie. Katharine Hepburn observed Jane practicing a dive over and over for a scene, and congratulated her on overcoming her fears. She also told Jane that "Hank Fonda" was like Spencer Tracey. Both men "made harsh remarks but didn't mean to hurt anyone."

As Yeats' progressed Ascendant went void-of-course between Aries and Taurus Rising (e.g. it made no aspects from either Sign) he wrote Lady Gregory that he was "losing his center;" that he could "feel it shifting."

During the Aries progression, Capricorns with Air and Fire planets often see a new marriage as an adventure. Like Jane Fonda when she married Ted Turner three years after her divorce from Hayden, many seem eager to take a chance on Life. The Aries cycle builds confidence.

However, with a preponderance of Earth and Water Natal planets, Capricorn Rising is more conservative. Less adventurous, they take longer to move on. On the whole, however, during the Aries progression, Capricorn exhibits a positive attitude towards learning new skills.

Taurus Rising
Establishing a firm foundation for "Act III, the Last Act"

Taurus, like Capricorn, is an Earth Sign. The progressed Mask forms a comfortable trine to the Rising Sign. It's a Fixed Sign; Capricorn Rising prefers to be settled now. The Irish bard with the Gemini Sun, for instance, was ready to *put down roots.* Jane Fonda speaks of missing her children while constantly on the move between Atlanta and Turner's various ranches.

Taurus enhances Capricorn's practicality. Yeats

had progressed into Taurus when he met Ezra Pound. Confident in himself as a poet, Yeats allowed young Pound to underline every abstract word in his poems, then removed them. He said he'd "become a romantic *realist*." The same year that he met Pound (1908,) his father moved permanently to New York City. As correspondents, the relationship became much easier relationship for them both. Distance offers perspective, and also freedom.

This progression brings out the talents of any Natal Taurus planets in the Fifth (Creativity; children) or Sixth (Health) Houses. Ruled by Aphrodite, Taurus seeks peace, love, warmth and companionship. After Yeats progressed into Taurus, he and Maud became reconciled as friends;[87] he proposed to Iseult and married Georgia ("George") Hyde-Lees. The late bloomer, having matured, decided that he wanted heirs.

During the early years of his marriage, Yeats restored an old tower named Thoor Ballylea.[88] In his poem of the same name, he claimed to have bought it for "my wife George," but his joy in a home that was also a piece of Irish history comes through the poem strongly.

---

87 1909.

88 In the mundane sense, buying a tower might symbolize the desire to "lord it over others;" to "look down upon one's land like a feudal lord." But in Yeats' case, the tower and the land around it were sold separately; he didn't own the surrounding pastures. Ellmann sees Yeats' poem, "The Winding Stairs" in *The Tower* collection as "an emblem of spiritual ascent," (cited above 143) and is probably more accurate.

Yeats in his early fifties, is a man of substance, a property owner in his natal place. Owning the tower meant that he was no longer a guest of friends, relatives, or his patroness, Lady Gregory, when he arrived from London. He now "belonged" in Ireland.

In the Taurus cycle, Capricorn appreciates nature. Located in the quiet countryside, the tower was far from Dublin political and theatrical intrigues, and Yeats could write in peace. Though the couple attended plays at the Abbey theater in Dublin and spent part of every year in London,[89] most of his writing and Georgia's automatic writing was done in the tower.[90]

Financial planning is featured in the Taurus progression. The least materialistic example in this chapter, Marie Curie, regretted not doing more for her country, Poland. Prescient, she "knew" that many useful radium-based discoveries lay ahead. She wanted to endow a lab in Crakow, but as she'd never patented her discoveries, she had no money to fund it.

In spite of her dislike of travel and speaking abroad, she went to the US to raise money during the Harding and Hoover administrations. She happily returned, once with $50,000 and once with a gram of radium, worth a fortune at the time, for the lab in Poland.

Taurus is also about comfort. During the first few years of Taurus, Capricorn Rising usually says, "I no longer want to live like a graduate student." They acquire

---

89 As a Senator, he eventually spent more time in Dublin.
90 At the end of his life, in "The Black Tower," Yeats wrote that the old king (Ego) no longer needed to defend his tower, it was time to send the soldiers away. Eventually, a new king would come to occupy it.

bigger homes and more comfortable cars. However, after a few years have passed, some of them resemble the Unicorn staring into the "Abyss of Materialism." (See "The Esoteric Ruler.") They complain about "high property taxes and insurance costs." Their yard becomes "too big to maintain." Everything seems too expensive. The astrologer hears, "things have gotten out-of-control! I want my life back!"

Children and grandchildren are usually seen as a great blessing during Taurus. As Capricorn Rising reaches what Jane Fonda called, "Act III, the Last Act," and the pace of their busy professional lives slows, many Capricorn Rising women wonder why they were always too busy to "really appreciate" their children.

During Taurus, several enjoyed making photograph albums for their descendants, or taking trips to research genealogy. Most of the women really enjoy spending time with grandchildren. Jane Fonda said her heart opened completely to her grandson, Matthew, in a way it had never opened before. Curie loved working in the lab with her daughter Irene and her son-in-law. Mead made an elaborate family tree for her grandchildren.

While some Capricorn Rising men enjoy spending time with grandchildren, others continue to put work (or golf) first. Some enjoy their involvement with a civic, religious or other voluntary organization, the Rotary, or Doctors without Borders. Accustomed to receiving praise and feeling fulfilled *outside the home,*[91] they continue in the same pattern.

Spirituality may become important to Capricorn Rising in this progression. For some, like Yeats, it's

91 House Ten is opposite House Four.

always been important while others, like Fonda, develop an interest around sixty, during the Jupiter Return.[92] And a few, like Art Buchwald, never seem to move past their cynical defenses.

The Gemini Progression - The Inconjunct

Gemini is Mutable Air and Mercury-ruled. Mentoring was a joy for Yeats (through his letters and prefaces,[93]) Mead (through her seminars,) and Curie (training her daughter and others in the lab; teaching at the Sorbonne.)

Yeats, Buchwald, Mead, and Bradbury all lived long enough to begin this progression. All of them were still working![94]

Mead, ignoring pancreatic cancer, continued to travel, speak, and write articles to the end. Her health worried others (her daughter, students, and sponsoring organizations,) more than it concerned Margaret herself.

"Inconjunct insights" open Capricorn's thinking

92 Though several years before that, she'd asked Ambassador Andrew Young what "being saved" meant. He told her the word "saved" meant "Whole" in Greek.

93 Like the one he wrote about writing for Lady Dorothy Wellesley.

94 Fonda, of course, is still alive. She'll be a progressed Taurus for many years to come. She's currently working with her foundation and performing in an "indie" film, in the role of a hippie grandmother estranged from the rest of the family.

to new people and ideas. Yeats helped Swami Purohit with several English translations, the life of the Swami's guru, the *Bhagavat Gita,* the *Upanisads* and the *Yoga Sutras.*

During this "Peter Pan" Gemini progression, Yeats also underwent "rejuvenation surgery," then seemed to return to puberty. Many younger women were drawn to the sexy, famous poet in his old age! Yeats was still writing and revising the week before his death.

Mead traveled to the Pacific islands and visited a young American anthropologist at work. Ever practical, she told villagers, "since disposable grass skirts have been replaced with cotton cloth, soap is essential!"

When interviewed on his eightieth birthday, Bradbury said he'd planned his work for the next twenty years." Forty short stories were underway, some of which were revisions of earlier attempts.

The inconjunct aspect is associated with surprises. Buchwald dictated his last book from hospice, surprised to have lived past everyone's expectations, including his own. He ended *Too Soon to Say Goodbye* with his friends' eulogies so that he could read and enjoy them before his death.

These Capricorn Rising examples were happily productive to their last breath. My older Capricorn Rising clients and friends seem to be following this pattern.

Capricorn Rising Bibliography

Avery, Jeanne, *The Rising Sign,* "Capricorn," (New York: Doubleday,) 1982.

Bailey, Alice A, *Esoteric Astrology,* "Capricorn," (New York: Lucis Press,) 1972.

Banner, Lois W., *Intertwined Lives: Margaret Mead, Ruth Benedict and their Circle,* (New York: Alfred A. Knopf,) 2003.

Bateson, Catherine, *With a Daughter's Eye, A Memoir of Margaret Mead and Gregory Bateson,* (New York: Harper Perennial,) 1984.

Buchwald, Art, *Too Soon to Say Goodbye,* (New York: Random House,) 2006.

Curie, Eve, *A Biography of Madame Curie,* trans, Vincent Sheean, (New York: Doubleday Doran,)1938, and (Cambridge: Da Capo Press,) 2001.

Ellmann, Richard, *Four Dubliners: Wilde, Yeats, Joyce and Beckett,* (Washington DC: Library of Congress,) 1987.

—— *Identity of Yeats,* (New York: Oxford University Press,) 1964

—— *Ulysses on the Liffey,* (New York: University Press,) 1972.

—— *Yeats: The Man and the Masks,* (New York: Norton,) 1979.

Fonda, Jane, *My Life So Far,* (New York: Random House,) 2006.

Foster, RE, *W.B. Yeats: A Life, I, The Apprentice Mage, 1865-*

1914, (Oxford: University Press,) 1998. (The "official" biography commissioned by the family.)

—— *W.B. Yeats: A Life, II, The Arch-Poet, 1915-1939,* (Oxford: University Press,) 2005.

Gorski, William T, *Yeats and Alchemy,* (Albany: SUNY Studies in the Western Esoteric Tradition,) 1996.

Hathaway, Nancy, *The Unicorn, (*New York: Viking Studio Books,) 1980.

Heindel, Max and August Foss, *The Message of the Stars,* (Oceanside: Rosicrucian Press,) 1980.

Henn, Thomas R, *The Lonely Tower: The Poetry of W.B. Yeats,* (New York: Methuen,) 1979.

Howard, Jane, *Margaret Mead: A Life, (*New York: Random House-Balantine,) 1984.

Kafka, Franz, "A Fable," in *The Transformation and Other Short Stories,* (New York: Penguin,) 1992.

Kinsley, James, ed, *The Poems and Fables of John Dryden, (*London: Oxford University Press,) 1963.

Maddox, Brenda, *Nora: The Real Life of Molly Bloom, (*Boston, Houghton Mifflin,) 1988.

McEvers, Joan, *12 Times 12: 144 Sun/Ascendant Combinations, (*San Diego: ACS,) 1983.

Mead, Margaret, *Blackberry Winter: My Earlier Years, (*New York: William Morrow and Co,) 1972.

—— *Letters from the Field 1925-1975,* (NY: Harper Perennial,) 2001.

—— *To Cherish the Life of the World: Selected Letters of*

Margaret Mead, Margaret Caffrey, ed, (New York: Basic Books,) 2006.

Moore, Virginia, *The Unicorn: W.B. Yeats' Search for Reality,* (New York: Macmillan,) 1954.

Pflaum, Rosalynd, *Grand Obsession: Madame Curie and Her World,* (New York: Doubleday,) 1989.

Raine, Kathleen, *Yeats the Initiate,* (London: Allan and Unwin,) 1986.

—— W.B. Yeats, *The Learning of the Imagination,* (Dallas: Institute of Leaning and Culture,) 2001.

Tolstoy, Leo, *The Death of Ivan Ilyich,* Lynn Solotaroff, trans, (New York: Bantam,) 1981.

Weller, Sam, *The Bradbury Chronicles: The Life of Ray Bradbury, Predicting the Past, Remembering the Future,* (New York: HarperCollins,) 2003.

Yeats, W.B., *The Collected Poems,* Richard J Finneran, ed, "Among School Children," "The Man and the Echo," "Lines Written in Dejection," "The Black Tower," (New York: Scribner, 1989).(SH)

—— *The Collected Works of W.B.Yeats: Prefaces and Introductions,* William H O'Donnell, ed, (New York: Macmillan,) 1989.

—— *Memoirs, with material not included in earlier editions,* Dennis Donoghue, ed, (London: Macmillan) 1977. Part II, astrology journal.

—— *The Gonne-Yeats Letters,* (New York: Syracuse University Press,) 1992. (The spiritual marriage; their synchronous dreams.)

—— *W.B. Yeats and Lady Augusta Gregory, ed, Kathleen*

Worth, "Where There is Nothing, There is God" and "The Unicorn from the Stars," plays (Washington DC: Catholic University of America Press,) 1987.

—— *A Vision,* (London: Macmillan,) 1926; 1956 eds.

Yogananda, Parmahansa, (Mukunda Lal Ghosh,) *Autobiography of a Yogi,* (Los Angeles: Self Realization Fellowship Press,) 1971.

You might also enjoy reading

Beyond the Mask: The Rising Sign - Part I & II
by Kathleen Burt ISBN 978-1-926975-08-5

The Creative Soul: Art and the Quest for Wholeness
by Lawrence Staples ISBN 978-0-9810344-4-7

The Guilt Cure by Pennington & Staples
ISBN 978-1-926715-53-7

Eros and the Shattering Gaze: Transcending Narcissism
by Ken Kimmel ISBN 978-1-926715-49-0

Divine Madness: Archetypes of Romantic Love
by John R. Haule ISBN 978-1-926715-04-9

Farming Soul: A Tale of Initiation
by Patricia Damery ISBN 978-1-926715-01-8

The Motherline: Every Woman's Journey to Find her Female Roots
by Naomi Ruth Lowinsky ISBN 978-0-9810344-6-1

The Sister From Below: When the Muse Gets Her Way
by Naomi Ruth Lowinsky ISBN 978-0-9810344-2-3

Becoming: An Introduction to Jung's Concept of Individuation
by Deldon Anne McNeely ISBN 978-1-926715-12-4

Made in United States
Orlando, FL
05 November 2026

90230155R00069